PUGLIA ITALY TRAVEL GUIDE 2023-2024

Insider Tips, Local Secrets And Unforgettable Experiences For Your Adventure In The Bread Basket Of Italy

D1716063

EVELYN BLAIR

Copyright © 2023 by Evelyn Blair

TABLE OF CONTENT

INTRODUCTION

Puglia is an alluring region, where a rich cultural heritage, stunning natural beauty, and ancient history coexist together. Prepare yourself to set out on a life-changing tour through the heart of Southern Italy's sun-drenched region as you hold this travel book in your hands. Do well to explore Puglia's undiscovered gems with its whitewashed villages, endless olive orchards, and blue lagoons.

We have created an immersive experience that goes beyond the ordinary and delves deeply into the character of this alluring region in this Puglia travel guide. Puglia has a lot to offer, whether you're an adventurous traveller looking for unusual experiences or a culture vulture wishing to experience real traditions.

Allow yourself to be charmed by the mouthwatering fragrances of Puglia's world-famous food, which includes velvety burrata cheese and tantalising orecchiette pasta. Experience the age-old customs of regional festivals that honour the region's colourful past, and get lost in the confusing lanes of historic towns where history has been whispered down the ages.

We've searched far and low for insider information, hidden gems, and local knowledge to help you make the most of your Puglian experience. Explore remote beaches, interact with craftspeople who are maintaining traditional techniques, and take pleasure in the straightforward pleasures of life that only Puglia can provide.

Allow your imagination to soar as you browse through these pages and let Puglia's allure work its magic on you. This book is your key to discovering Puglia, whether you're planning a solo journey, a romantic retreat, or an exciting family trip.

So gather your belongings, enjoy the warmth of the Apulian sun, and start your journey. When you arrive, Puglia is eager to charm, enthral, and leave a lasting impression on your heart. Together, let's discover the remarkable in Puglia, Italy's enduringly alluring region!

CHAPTER 1

Italy's Timeless Charmer

Geography and Location

Puglia is a beautiful region blessed with varied landscapes, a rich history, and a distinctive cultural legacy. It is located in the sun-drenched heel of Italy's famous boot. It is a bridge connecting Europe and the East thanks to its advantageous location in Southern Italy as an entrance to the Mediterranean. This part of this book will explore the geological marvels and distinctive locations that have moulded Puglia's charm and contributed to its reputation as a must-visit location.

The Majesty of the Mediterranean

Puglia has a long, stunning coastline that stretches over 800 km along the glistening Adriatic and Ionian Seas. Travellers can enjoy a wide variety of coastal experiences in this majestic region of the Mediterranean, from the craggy cliffs and secret coves of the Gargano Peninsula to the sandy beaches and clear waters of Salento.

Find the pristine beaches of Torre Lapillo and Punta Prosciutto, famed for their white sands and inviting shallows, or explore the dramatic sea caves of

Polignano a Mare, where turquoise waters crash against limestone cliffs. Each coastal town and village has its own unique appeal, offering a variety of aquatic adventures, mouthwatering seafood treats, and spellbinding vistas.

The Itria Valley

With its famous trulli cottages dotting the landscape amid endless olive trees and vineyards, the Itria Valley in the interior unfolds like a scene from a novel. The pinnacle of this captivating region, whose whitewashed, cone-shaped buildings form a scene straight out of a storybook, is Alberobello, a UNESCO World Heritage site.

You'll come across charming communities like Locorotondo and Cisternino, each with its own special charm and personality, as you meander through this enchanted valley. In addition to being aesthetically beautiful, the olive trees that dot the landscape also yield some of Italy's best olive oils, which play a crucial role in Puglia's culinary heritage.

The Murge Plateau

The Murge Plateau, a huge area of limestone that gives the scenery a distinctive, rustic character, graces Central Puglia. This area is dotted with historical landmarks and archaeological wonders, like the spectacular Castel del Monte, a fortress from the 13th century known for its unusual octagonal shape, and the enigmatic rock-cut cathedrals of Matera, a nearby city in Basilicata.

The Murge Plateau is a hiker and nature lover's heaven, offering expansive views, luxuriant meadows of wildflowers, and the opportunity to see local fauna. Discover the beautiful griffon vulture in the Alta Murgia National Park, a protected area that is home to many bird species.

The Salento Peninsula

The gorgeous Salento Peninsula, located south of Puglia, is recognised for its pristine scenery and rich cultural legacy. A remarkable fusion of Greek, Roman, and Byzantine influences can be seen in the architecture, customary celebrations, and regional dialect of the Salento region.

Lecce, dubbed the "Florence of the South," is noted for its stunning baroque architecture, which is evidence of the area's artistic talent. The Cape of Santa Maria di Leuca, where the Adriatic and Ionian Seas converge to provide an amazing natural spectacle, is located further south.

Puglia's Strategic Position, the Mediterranean Gateway

The geographic setting of Puglia has long had a considerable impact on its history and culture.

Puglia has always served as a crossroads for trade and cross-cultural contact because of its location. The architecture, gastronomy, and customs of the area have the unmistakable imprint of the influences of the Greeks, Romans, Byzantines, Normans, and many more.

Additionally, Puglia's proximity to the Mediterranean has helped to build its reputation as a nation of fishermen and seafarers. Its ports have fostered interactions with neighbouring nations and given its renowned agricultural products a platform for export.

Puglia's geography plays a key role in the appeal of the region as a tourism destination. Puglia is a really enchanted location just waiting to be discovered because of its varied landscapes, stunning coastline, historical treasures, and cultural melting pot.

Climate and Weather

Planning an enjoyable and comfortable trip to this Mediterranean treasure requires having an understanding of Puglia's environment and weather. Puglia, which enjoys a typical Mediterranean environment with mild winters, sunny summers, and nice shoulder seasons, makes a great year-round vacation spot for tourists looking for a variety of activities. Here, we'll discuss seasonal changes, temperature ranges, and the ideal times to visit each magical location in this Italian paradise.

Spring in Bloom (March through May)

Puglia's springtime is a sensory joy as the countryside awakens with vivid hues and invigorating aromas. With moderate weather and blooming almond trees, March heralds the season of rebirth and the change from winter to spring. As April approaches, the countryside blooms with wildflowers and the weather progressively gets warmer, making outdoor activities enjoyable.

Puglia is best visited in May, when average temperatures range from 17°C to 24°C (63°F to 75°F). The beaches become more appealing for early swimmers as the Mediterranean Sea begins to warm up. A great time to visit lovely towns and rural areas without the heaviest tourist traffic is in the spring.

Summer Bliss (June to August)

Puglia's summer season offers the traditional Mediterranean experience with warm evenings and sunny days. The weather is nice in June, with average highs and lows of 26°C and 30°C (79°F and 86°F). As July and August approach, the heat increases and highs of 30°C to 35°C (86°F to 95°F) are not uncommon.

These months are ideal for water lovers and beachgoers because the sea is at its hottest. Beach parties, outdoor festivals, and a thriving nightlife bring the coastal resort towns and cities to life. However, during the hottest parts of the summer, it's critical to maintain hydration and use sun protection measures.

The Golden Glow of Autumn (September to November)

Due to the region's golden colour and the start of the harvest season, autumn is a lovely time of year in Puglia. With average temperatures between 25°C and 29°C (77°F and 84°F), September is still a great month for outdoor activities on the beach and discovering the treasures of the interior.

As October approaches, the temperatures steadily drop, making the weather ideal for outdoor activities like sightseeing. During this time, olive harvesting takes centre stage, providing a distinctive opportunity to observe traditional practises and sample the most recent olive oils.

Winter (December to February)

Puglia has moderate winters in comparison to several other European countries. The coldest months are December and January, when average highs range from 8°C to 14°C (46°F to 57°F). While snowfall is uncommon, this time of year the area can see several rainy days.

Even in the winter, Puglia retains its allure despite the lower temperatures. Christmas and New Year celebrations are lively, with cities decked out in holiday lights and annual activities held to commemorate the season.

The Ideal Season to Visit Puglia

Your interests and intended experiences will ultimately determine the ideal time to visit Puglia. June to September are the best months to soak up the sun and savour the seaside beauty if you appreciate the buzzy atmosphere of summer and beach activities. However, the shoulder seasons of spring and fall are great for visitors looking for milder temperatures and a more laid-back atmosphere, with May and September presenting a sweet spot of pleasant weather and fewer crowds.

Visitors looking for a variety of experiences will find Puglia to be a delight all year round because of its Mediterranean climate. Puglia's temperature and weather make it a timeless location ready to be discovered, whether you're drawn to sun-kissed beaches, scented vineyards, or old historical ruins.

Customs and Norms

Time-honored traditions, vibrant customs, and a rich cultural heritage constitute the very foundation of identity in the sun-drenched region of Puglia. This guide allows you to become fully immersed in the rich fabric of Puglia's traditions and culture, which have been shaped by a confluence of influences from ancient civilizations, invasions, and interactions with neighbouring nations.

Puglians are well known for their generous hospitality and sincere kindness. Strong ties to others and a sense of belonging are fundamental components of the local culture. The people of Puglia take pride in sharing their culture, customs, and tales with visitors, and they do so with open arms.

You'll probably be invited to take part in regional celebrations, get-togethers, and family meals while visiting Puglia. If you adopt this attitude of openness and acceptance, you'll surely develop enduring relationships with the locals.

Puglia's rich cultural legacy also includes the mesmerising traditional dance known as the Tarantella, which has its roots in Southern Italy. Traditional music using instruments like accordions, mandolins, and tambourines is frequently played to accompany this vivacious and rhythmic dance.

You will be able to see the captivating Tarantella performances at special events and festivals. Don't be afraid to participate in the dance; the locals will be happy to show you the moves and share the joy of this long-standing custom.

Puglia's rich history and many influences are reflected in the region's architectural environment. With their conical roofs and whitewashed walls, trulli cottages are a symbol of the area's uniqueness. The biggest number of these distinctive buildings may be seen in Alberobello, a UNESCO World Heritage site.

The towns of Lecce, Martina Franca, and Gallipoli, on the other hand, are examples of beautiful baroque architecture that is embellished with elaborate carvings and ornamental façade. These towns' streets are like walking through a time machine, with stunning architecture around every bend.

Puglia's strong coastal heritage and abundant agricultural heritage form the foundation of its culinary traditions. The area is referred to as the "breadbasket of Italy" since it produces a large quantity of wine, olive oil, and cereals. The food of Puglia is known for its straightforward but tasty recipes that frequently include local seafood and fresh veggies.

A typical Puglian cuisine is orecchiette pasta, which is typically served with a variety of sauces. Enjoy the mouthwatering burrata cheese, which is oozing with creamy richness, and the flavorful stews made with robust meats and vegetables that are typical of the area. Don't forget to drink a glass of the well-regarded Primitivo or Negroamaro wine with your meals.

Puglia is home to talented craftspeople who uphold traditional techniques and produce one-of-a-kind handmade goods. Visit the artisan studios to see the pottery, weaving, and woodcarving arts in action. Particularly well-known for their ceramics, Puglia produces exquisite pottery that is decorated with elaborate patterns and vivid colours.

Puglia's traditions and culture offer a fascinating tapestry of customs, festivals, and artistic manifestations that have endured through the ages. Experience the welcoming warmth of southern hospitality, the delectable flavours of its cuisine, and the exuberant energy of its festivals. You'll develop a stronger bond with Puglia as you learn more about its traditions and culture, developing treasured experiences that will last a lifetime.

CHAPTER 2

The Cities and Towns of Puglia

Puglia, an alluring region in the heel of Italy's boot, is home to a wealth of historical landmarks, cultural treasures, and spectacular natural beauty. Every town and city in Puglia has its own distinct charm and appeal, providing visitors with a varied and educational experience.

Bari

Bari, the capital of Puglia, is a bustling port city that skillfully combines the past with the present. Bari Vecchia, the city's historic core, is a labyrinth of winding lanes, antique churches, and attractive public spaces. Explore the eerie alleyways to find the Basilica di San Nicola, a holy place where Saint Nicholas' remains are kept. At the crowded fish market, where the freshest catch is on display, embrace the way of life in the area.

A modern contrast may be found in Bari's new town, which features opulent boulevards, chic shops, and a bustling nightlife. Enjoy delectable seafood delicacies at the waterfront eateries while strolling along the coastal promenade. The neighbouring villages of Polignano a Mare and Monopoli, both known for their seaside beauty and historical charm, may be reached from Bari as well.

Lecce

Lecce, known for its lavish Baroque architecture, is frequently called the "Florence of the South." The Basilica di Santa Croce and Piazza del Duomo serve as prominent examples of this magnificent design in the city's historic centre, which is a masterpiece of complex stone carvings and beautiful facades. Take a stroll around the bustling streets while indulging in some of the delicious pasticciotto, a local custard-filled pastry.

Lecce has a thriving cultural environment, with theatres, galleries, and craft studios showing the locals' artistic abilities. After sunset, clubs and cafes overflow into the streets as the city comes to life with a vibrant nightlife. Lecce's centre location in Salento makes it a great starting point for visiting the region's gorgeous villages and sun-kissed beaches.

Alberobello

Alberobello is a special place that transports tourists to a world of trulli houses, classic stone homes with cone-shaped roofs, that resembles something out of a fantasy. A UNESCO World Heritage site, Alberobello's Trulli, produces an unearthly atmosphere that appeals to the imagination. Explore the trulli zone at your leisure to find quaint boutiques, eateries, and regional artists.

With rolling vineyards and olive trees dotting the landscape, Alberobello provides a glimpse of rural Puglian life outside of the trulli zone. Visit nearby vineyards and farms to taste the region's world-famous wines and olive oils. Any Puglia travel itinerary should include a stay at Alberobello because of its magical environment.

Ostuni

Ostuni, a shining gem in Puglia's crown perched atop a hill, has earned the moniker "White City." A picturesque scene is created by the town's whitewashed structures, winding streets, and breathtaking Adriatic Sea vistas. Discover the historic center's winding lanes, where tiny stores and artisan boutiques tempt you.

Locally produced wines, seafood specialties, and olive oil are among Ostuni's culinary delights. The rich flavours of the area's land and sea are reflected in the town's culinary traditions. Don't pass up the opportunity to enjoy a typical Puglian lunch at a nearby trattoria.

Gallipoli

Gallipoli, a beachfront jewel with sandy beaches and crystal-clear waters, is situated on the Ionian coast. On a small island, the old centre is a walled labyrinth of winding streets, historic churches, and breathtaking sea vistas. The thriving fish market and seafood eateries that line the harbour show the town's history as a fishing community.

There are numerous sandy coves and immaculate beaches around the coast of Gallipoli, adding to the city's coastal attractiveness outside of the ancient district. Take advantage of the sea and sun, or go on boat cruises to see the neighbouring caverns and undiscovered coves.

Polignano a Mare

Polignano a Mare is a breath-taking town that puts visitors in amazement. It is perched atop limestone cliffs overlooking the turquoise seas of the Adriatic Sea. The town's stunning white buildings and dramatic coastline location combine to create a magical ambience. Discover the breathtaking views from the balconies along the cliffside as you stroll through the winding alleyways.

The beaches and coves in Polignano a Mare provide chances for swimming, cliff diving, and tanning. For a special dinner with breathtaking views of the ocean, you must go to the Grotta Palazzese restaurant, which is located inside a sea cave.

Monopoli

The coastal town of Monopoli, which is nestled along the Adriatic Sea, is known for its marine appeal and has a long history as an important port in antiquity. A picture-perfect scenario is created by the town's defensive walls, mediaeval castle, and lovely harbour. Discover hidden treasures like the Cathedral of Santa Maria della Madia and the Castle of Charles V as you meander through the cobblestoned streets of the old centre.

The vibrant fish market, where local fishermen sell their catch of the day, honours Monopoli's thriving fishing sector. Enjoy the delicious seafood meals served in the area, such as savoury seafood pasta and freshly grilled salmon. Don't pass up the chance to unwind on one of Monopoli's sandy beaches or go on a boat excursion to see the breathtaking sea caves and rock formations.

Martina Franca

Martina Franca, a Baroque treasure hidden in the scenic Valle d'Itria, charms visitors with its exquisite architecture and welcoming ambiance. The town's old district is home to stunning palaces, elaborate churches, and balconies with elaborate decorations. Investigate the bustling Piazza del Plebiscito, which is flanked by quaint shops and cafes.

The yearly Festival della Valle d'Itria, which honours opera and classical music, is one of the many cultural events held in Martina Franca. Travellers are invited to explore the bucolic sceneries of the Valle d'Itria by the lovely countryside and quaint trulli that dot the area.

Trani

Located on the seaside, Trani is a beautiful city with a long history. Saint Nicholas the Pilgrim is honoured at the city's magnificent Romanesque church, which sits magnificently by the water and provides breathtaking sunset views. Take a stroll around the harbour promenade and take in the beautiful fishing vessels and luxurious yachts.

The town's historical district is home to quaint streets, grand palaces, and welcoming piazzas. Experience the famed Trani mussels, a regional speciality that honours the town's marine past. Trani is a charming coastal destination in Puglia because of its stunning seaside setting and architectural gems.

Cisternino

Cisternino, a timeless village with classic trulli homes and whitewashed structures, is perched atop a hill in the Valle d'Itria. The town's old district is a maze of winding lanes where tourists can take in the straightforward beauty of the stone construction. View the surrounding landscape in its entirety from the town's belvedere.

Famous for its grilled meat dishes, Cisternino is known for its flavorful "bombette"—thinly sliced meat coated in cheese and spices. Savour the flavours of the regional cuisine while having a leisurely supper at one of the cosy trattorias. The serene atmosphere and picturesque surroundings of Cisternino provide a peaceful haven in the middle of Puglia.

Vieste

Vieste, a seaside paradise with beautiful beaches, towering cliffs, and a rich historical past, is located on the breathtaking Gargano Peninsula along the Adriatic coast. Its lovely old town, clean waters, and jaw-dropping sea caves make this quaint hamlet in the province of Foggia a popular vacation spot for beachgoers, nature lovers, and history aficionados alike. The ideal fusion of natural beauty, cultural richness, and a laid-back coastal atmosphere found in Vieste entices visitors to discover its charms.

Fasano

Fasano is a lovely hamlet that perfectly combines its rich historical past with the attractiveness of the adjacent Adriatic Sea. It is located in the Itria Valley. Fasano provides visitors with a trip back in time and the chance to take in the coastal beauty of Puglia thanks to its stunning landscapes, historic sites, and traditional architecture. Fasano entices visitors to discover its varied attractions and immerse themselves in the true atmosphere of this alluring town with its opulent palaces, traditional trulli homes, sandy beaches, and nature preserves.

Elegant mansions, antique churches, and quaint squares can be found throughout Fasano's historic centre, which is a historical treasure trove. The town's illustrious past and rich architectural heritage are attested to by the Palazzo del Bal, a stunning palace from the 16th century.

An additional significant landmark that highlights the town's artistic and theological significance is the Church of San Giovanni Battista, which has a stunning Baroque facade. Visitors can take in the atmosphere of the past as they meander around the little streets and take in the town's well-preserved architectural treasures.

Travellers are invited to explore Fasano's rich legacy, savour the coastal splendour, and take in the genuine charm of Puglia where history meets the sea. Fasano provides a wide range of events that perfectly capture the spirit of this alluring town, from its historical landmarks to its sandy beaches and animal adventures.

Exploring the towns and cities of Puglia is a voyage through time and culture because each one of them has its own history to share. Each place encourages travellers to experience the true spirit of Puglia.

Discover the hidden jewels and well-known attractions of Puglia's cities and towns as you eat your way through the native food, take in the scenery, and become immersed in the local customs. Let the magic unfold before you as you set off on an extraordinary adventure through Puglia from the busy city to the tranquil countryside.

CHAPTER 3

Transportation

One secret to effortlessly enjoying Puglia's treasures is effective and dependable transportation. This chapter will be your guide to the various modes of transport offered in the area as you journey through the sun-drenched landscapes, ancient towns, and picturesque coastlines, ensuring you can travel easily and make the most of your Puglian adventure.

Arriving in Puglia

Due to its excellent connectivity to important Italian and European towns, Puglia is a popular travel destination for tourists from throughout the globe.

By Air

The first step in starting a memorable adventure across Italy's sun-kissed paradise is flying into Puglia. The two main airports in Puglia, Bari Karol Wojtyła Airport (BRI) and Brindisi Papola Casale Airport (BDS), act as entry points for tourists from all over the world. We'll cover everything you need to know about getting into Puglia by air,, from airline options and airport amenities to ground transportation and the exhilaration of starting your Puglian journey.

Bari Karol Wojtyła Airport (BRI)

Puglia's main international airport, Bari Airport, which bears Pope John Paul II (Karol Wojtyła)'s name, is situated about 8 kilometres (5 miles) northwest of the city of Bari. Travellers arriving from numerous European and international locations use it as their primary entrance point. The airport offers both local and international service, making it simple to reach from the country's largest cities as well as from other countries.

Brindisi Papola Casale Airport (BDS)

Brindisi Papola Casale Airport, also referred to as Brindisi Airport, is located around 6 kilometres (4 miles) from the city of Brindisi. It offers internal and international service, connecting Puglia to a number of European cities, like Bari Airport does. Travellers going to Puglia's southernmost region, the Salento Peninsula, will find Brindisi Airport to be particularly handy.

Global Connectivity

There are numerous important European cities, like London, Paris, Munich, Barcelona, and Amsterdam, that may be reached directly from the airports of Bari and Brindisi. Additionally, they accommodate seasonal flights from numerous other foreign locations, giving tourists more options to choose from during the busiest travel times.

Domestic Flights

The major Italian cities of Rome, Milan, Venice, Florence, and Naples all have direct flights to and from Puglia's airports on a regular basis. Puglia is easily accessible from any region of Italy, making it a favourite vacation spot for Italian citizens as well.

Airport Services and Amenities

The airports in Bari and Brindisi offer travellers cutting-edge amenities and services to ensure a comfortable journey. Both airports include a variety of services, such as shops, eateries, cafes, and duty-free shops, enabling travellers to unwind and have a good time while they wait for their flights.

Ground Transportation from the Airports

Travellers can choose from a variety of modes of transportation to get to their selected destinations in Puglia from the airports in Bari and Brindisi:

- Rental Vehicles
Both airports include car rental companies, allowing visitors the option to explore Puglia at their own speed. Those who want to take road trips and

discover the area's hidden jewels may consider renting a car.

- Taxis and Airport Shuttles
Travellers may easily get to the major towns and cities in Puglia via shuttle buses and taxis. While taxis offer greater flexibility and convenience, shuttle services frequently adhere to set schedules.

- Services for Trains
The close train stations at the airports in Bari and Brindisi provide quick access to numerous locations within Puglia and beyond.

- Public Buses
Public buses connect the airports to other towns and cities, offering tourists an affordable mode of transit.

Information about Immigration and Visas

For brief visits, visitors arriving in Puglia by air from Schengen Area nations typically do not need a visa. However, before visiting Italy, it's important to confirm the laws and restrictions regarding visas based on your nationality.

Banking and Currency Exchange Services

Both airports provide ATMs and foreign exchange desks, enabling visitors to obtain Euros for their costs while visiting Puglia.

Air travel to Puglia opens the door to Italy's sun-drenched paradise, where mesmerising scenery, a rich history, and gracious hospitality are waiting. Whether you land at Brindisi Papola Casale Airport or Bari Karol Wojtya Airport, you'll immediately feel the appeal of Puglia's charm as soon as your feet touch this magical Italian soil. Your trip to Puglia is guaranteed to be seamless and extraordinary thanks to the up-to-date airport amenities and practical ground transportation alternatives.

By Rail

Getting to Puglia by rail is a beautiful and relaxing way to experience the area's alluring landscapes and ancient cities. The well-connected rail system in Puglia makes it simple to travel there by train from significant Italian cities and other regions. We'll cover all you need to know about taking the train to Puglia from important train stations to well-traveled routes, ensuring you have a smooth and enjoyable trip to this magical region of Italy.

Puglian Major Train Stations

There are numerous significant train stations in Puglia that are important places of arrival and departure for tourists:

- Bari Centrale

One of Puglia's major railway hubs is the principal train station in Bari, which is situated right in the middle of the city. It links Bari to a number of locations both locally and across Italy.

- Lecce Stazione
The Salento Peninsula may be reached via the primary train station in Lecce, which also provides links to well-liked locations in southern Puglia.

- Brindisi Centrale
The Salento Peninsula is easily accessible from Brindisi's central train station, which also acts as a key interchange for visitors coming from other regions of Italy.

- Foggia Centrale
The central train station in Foggia is an important transit hub for visitors coming from northern Italy and other areas.

Fast Trains to Puglia

Major Italian cities are easily accessible from Puglia via the high-speed rail system. Trenitalia's Frecciarossa and Frecciargento trains provide quick and effective access to Puglia from Rome, Milan, Florence, and other important cities.

For instance, the Frecciarossa train travels through the Italian countryside in comfort and style in about 3 to 3.5 hours from Rome to Bari.

Regional Train Connections

The different towns and cities of Puglia can be explored at a slower pace by taking regional trains. Regional trains connecting major cities like Bari, Lecce, Brindisi, and Taranto to smaller towns and seaside locations are run by the Ferrovie del Sud Est (FSE) and Trenitalia networks.

By travelling through olive orchards, vineyards, and quaint rural areas, regional trains let you take in the stunning scenery of Puglia.

Well-liked Train Routes to Puglia

Popular train routes to Puglia include:

- Rome to Bari: This route provides a direct link between the bustling regional centre of Puglia, Bari, and the Italian capital, Rome.

- Naples to Bari: From Naples to Bari, travellers can take a beautiful coastal drive that passes through charming towns like Castellana Grotte and Polignano a Mare.

- Milan to Bari: This route links the vibrant city of Milan with the quaint villages and Puglian coasts.

Onboard Amenities & Comfort

Italian high-speed trains like the Frecciarossa and Frecciargento provide spacious seating, plenty of legroom, Wi-Fi, and catering options. Regional trains offer a leisurely and genuine travel experience that allows travellers to mingle with locals and experience the unique character of the region.

Train Reservations and Tickets

To reserve your desired travel schedule and seating, it is preferable to purchase rail tickets in advance, especially for high-speed trains. Tickets can be purchased at Italian train stations or online through the Trenitalia website.

Reservations are typically not necessary for regional trains, and you can buy tickets online or at ticket kiosks.

Arrival and Ground Transportation

You can easily take ground transportation to get to your lodging or other desired location after arriving at the Puglia train station of your choice:

- Taxis and car rentals: Taxis are easily found at train stations, offering a practical way to get to your lodging. For individuals who want to explore Puglia at their own pace, car rental companies are also present at the main train stations.

- Public Buses: Local buses frequently link train stations to neighbouring towns and cities, providing travellers with affordable transit options.

Getting to Puglia by train is a picturesque and enjoyable journey that lets you take in the natural beauty of Italy's countryside and the unique culture of the area. Train travel offers a seamless and immersive method to access this magical area of Italy, whether you're using high-speed trains from major Italian cities or experiencing Puglia's villages and coastal locations via regional trains. As your trip gets underway, sit back, unwind, and take it all in. Puglia's sun-drenched landscapes and rich legacy are waiting for you.

Getting Around Puglia

Public transit in Puglia is effective and well-managed, making it a practical choice for getting about the region's towns and cities. Buses connect even the tiniest villages to the major towns, making them the dominant form of public transit. There are bus services that run on set timetables and provide pleasant transportation for both urban and regional areas.

Trains are a common option for lengthier trips between large cities. Trains connecting Bari, Lecce, Brindisi, and other important locations are run by the Trenitalia and Ferrovie del Sud Est (FSE) networks. The train routes offer a convenient and lovely means of transportation while showcasing the natural beauty of Puglia's countryside.

For those who want flexibility and independence when travelling, renting a car is a great choice. The well-maintained road system in Puglia connects towns, cities, and tourist attractions, making it simple to see the area at your own speed. Major automobile rental firms have locations in major cities and at airports, offering a selection of vehicles to suit your needs.

Driving in Puglia gives you the freedom to go off the main road and find undiscovered jewels that may be difficult to reach by public transit. Additionally, it creates the possibility for leisurely drives along the coast or through lovely countryside.

Biking and walking are excellent alternatives for eco-conscious tourists and outdoor enthusiasts to get up close and personal with Puglia's scenery. You can enjoy the beauty of the countryside and fully immerse yourself in the region's genuine charm thanks to the network of bike routes and walking trails that the area has to offer.

Biking and walking trips provide a closer connection to Puglia's natural and cultural history, whether you choose to cycle along the antiquated Via Traiana, go on a walking tour of the lovely towns, or hike through the Gargano National Park.

Navigating the Islands of Puglia, through Ferries and Boat Tours

Tremiti Islands (Isole Tremiti) and Gallipoli on the Salento Peninsula are two stunning islands that may be found in Puglia. Ferries leave from Termoli in Molise and Vieste in Puglia for the Tremiti Islands. These magnificent islands provide a tranquil getaway from the mainland, crystal-clear waters, and fascinating aquatic life.

The Ionian Coast destination Gallipoli is a well-liked travel destination that can be reached by car, but you can also take boat cruises around the coast to get a different view of Puglia's marine splendour.

Important Transport Advice

- Prepare Ahead: Especially during the busiest travel times, check transportation timetables and reserve tickets in advance.

- Valid Documents: If you intend to rent a vehicle, be sure your driver's licence is up to date. Have your tickets and identification ready for rail travel.

- Parking: If you plan to drive in a city, familiarise yourself with the parking rules. Some regions have restricted parking zones or charge for parking.

- Public Transport Passes: If you frequently take public transport, you might want to get a regional transport pass for convenience and financial savings.

- Respect Local Customs: To ensure a nice experience for everyone, respect local customs and etiquette when driving or utilising public transit.

Navigating Puglia is a simple and delightful experience, thanks to an effective transit network and a variety of options to meet any traveler's preferences. Whether you decide to travel around Puglia by vehicle, boat, bicycle, or public transportation, each method of mobility offers a different perspective on the region's alluring landscapes, history, and culture. Plan ahead, enjoy the freedom to explore, and get ready to travel across the captivating south of Puglia and beyond.

CHAPTER 4

Accommodation in Puglia

Accommodation Types

Finding the ideal lodging is essential to make your trip to Puglia truly memorable as you travel through this alluring region. Puglia provides a wide range of lodging choices, from opulent seaside resorts to rustic Masserie (farmhouses) in the countryside and boutique hotels tucked away in charming old villages. We'll go over the different sorts of lodging in this chapter, helping you locate the ideal retreat to relax in and savour Puglia's alluring charm.

Luxurious Beach Resorts

Some of Italy's most opulent beach resorts may be found along Puglia's sun-drenched coastline. These breathtaking resorts provide easy access to immaculate beaches, clear waters, and first-rate facilities. Imagine yourself soaking up the Mediterranean sun, relaxing beside infinity pools that look out over the ocean, and treating yourself to spa services that calm your senses.

Popular seaside towns like Polignano a Mare, Monopoli, and Ostuni are home to a number of opulent beach resorts that each provide a little piece of heaven with stunning coastal views. You can be sure that these resorts offer the ideal balance of luxury and relaxation so that your visit will be filled with priceless memories.

Masseria

Consider staying in a Masseria, a typical farmhouse that has been transformed into delightful lodging, for a singular and genuine experience. Masserie are perfect for individuals looking for a close connection to Puglia's agricultural past because they combine rustic elegance, tradition, and rural tranquility.

Masserie is a tranquil setting for rest and exploration amid luscious vineyards and olive trees. Fresh local ingredients are used to construct farm-to-table meals, and you can also take part in activities like culinary workshops, wine tastings, and bike tours through the beautiful countryside.

Boutique Hotels

The charming boutique hotels in Puglia's ancient towns each provide a one-of-a-kind and customised experience. These little lodgings are frequently tucked away in centuries-old structures, radiating charm and character that honours the town's history.

Boutique hotels in cities like Lecce, Alberobello, and Gallipoli combine contemporary amenities with ancient architecture to give guests a sense of exclusivity and timelessness. Enjoy a leisurely breakfast in a charming courtyard as you awake to views of old passageways before venturing out to discover the town's cultural gems.

Agriturismo

Agriturismo, or farm stays, provide visitors a genuine flavour of rural and agricultural Puglian culture. These lodgings are often functioning farms that invite visitors to enjoy the ease and beauty of rural life.

When you stay at an agriturismo, you may enjoy excellent home-cooked meals created with farm-fresh ingredients and develop a connection to the land by participating in activities like harvesting, culinary workshops, and animal care. It's a great option for individuals who enjoy the outdoors and want to immerse themselves in the local culture.

Villas and Apartment Rentals

Apartment rentals and villas are great choices for travellers looking for more freedom and room. These lodgings, which can be found in historic districts, rural areas, or coastal towns, give you a home away from home so you can truly experience local culture.

While villas frequently include private pools and gardens, making them ideal for families or gatherings of friends, flat rentals provide you the freedom to cook your meals using fresh local ingredients. During your visit to Puglia, take advantage of the flexibility to choose your own schedule and live like a local.

Important Accommodation Advice

- Advance reservations
 This is advised to ensure your preferred choice of lodging during the busiest travel times.

- Proximity to Attractions
Take into account how close your lodging is to the sights and activities you want to see.

- Amenities and Services
Pay attention to the amenities and services provided by the lodging, and make sure they meet your needs and preferences.

- Authenticity and Experience
Opt for lodging that fits your vacation preferences, whether they be for luxury, rustic charm, or a mix of relaxation and cultural immersion.

- Cultural Immersion

Select lodgings that provide distinctive cultural encounters so you may get to know Puglia's history and customs.

Every traveller can find the ideal retreat in Puglia thanks to the variety of lodging alternatives available. No matter what kind of accommodation you're looking for—luxury, rustic charm, historical ambiance, or a mix of culture and relaxation, Puglia's lodgings will wow you with their distinctive charm and kind welcome. During your visit to Puglia, pick your ideal retreat, relax in its alluring surroundings, and make priceless memories.

Best Places for Luxurious Accommodations

The opulent housing options in Puglia cater to discerning tourists looking for the ideal fusion of grandeur, elegance, and genuine Italian charm. Puglia offers a variety of options that ensure an enjoyable stay, whether you're seeking for opulent coastal resorts, charming boutique hotels, or mediaeval Masseria converted into high-end sanctuaries. We will look at some of the top spots for opulent accomodation in Puglia where every moment is a celebration of sophistication and extravagance.

Polignano a Mare

With its stunning coastline views and extensive cultural history, Polignano a Mare provides a variety of opulent lodgings that perfectly capture elegance and richness. In this section of this book, we feature a hand-picked list of some of the most prestigious and sought-after brands in luxurious lodging in Polignano a Mare. Each of these luxurious villas offers an unrivalled beach experience by fusing elegant decor, top-notch amenities, and breathtaking Adriatic Sea views.

Grotta Palazzese Hotel

In Polignano a Mare, the Grotta Palazzese Hotel, a legendary name in opulent lodging, is housed inside a stunning natural cave. Guests at this renowned hotel may enjoy gourmet cuisine while perched on a balcony that soars above the ocean, providing an unmatched dining experience.

The artistically decorated rooms and suites at the Grotta Palazzese include private balconies with mesmerising views of the sea and the cave's magical innards. In this hotel, the charm of Puglia's seaside beauty melds perfectly with the mystery of the old cave, offering a one-of-a-kind and unforgettable experience.

Borgobianco Resort & Spa MGallery Hotel Collection

The Borgobianco Resort & Spa MGallery Hotel Collection is perched on a hilltop with a view of the Adriatic and emanates an aura of tranquilly and classic luxury. This classy 5-star resort boasts whitewashed structures, a gorgeously planted pool area, and chic interiors that pay homage to the local style of architecture.

The resort's wellness centre offers a variety of luxurious treatments and therapies, while the spacious and elegantly decorated suites give panoramic views of the ocean. The gourmet restaurant in Borgobianco features elegant Puglian food that highlights the area's gastronomic charms. This resort is a refuge of refinement in Polignano a Mare for people looking for a private and opulent getaway.

Cala Ponte Hotel

The Cala Ponte Hotel is an opulent facility that combines cutting-edge design with gracious service. It is located on the Polignano a Mare cliffs. The hotel's suites provide upscale furniture and modern conveniences, and many have their own balconies with breathtaking views of the Adriatic.

The rooftop terrace of the Cala Ponte Hotel is the ideal place to unwind, including a welcoming pool area and a bar that provides energising cocktails while overlooking the ocean. The hotel's restaurant provides guests opulent dining experiences with a fusion of traditional Puglian flavours and cutting-edge culinary inventions.

Pietrablu Resort & Spa

A haven of elegance and peace in Polignano a Mare, the Pietrablu Resort & Spa is surrounded by lush gardens and has a sea view. Private balconies or terraces in the resort's roomy, well decorated accommodations offer mesmerising views of the Adriatic Sea.

The spa at Pietrablu is a haven of tranquility, providing a variety of treatments that are inspired by Puglia's natural resources. The resort's restaurant emphasises fresh seafood and locally sourced products to highlight the region's culinary heritage. Pietrablu Resort & Spa provides a dreamy coastal hideaway in one of Puglia's most stunning places, with direct access to a private beach.

San Michele Suite & SPA

The San Michele Suite & SPA is an intimate and luxurious outique hotel tucked away in the centre of Polignano a Mare's historical district. The property's attractively constructed suites offer a fusion of contemporary comfort and historic charm and are decorated with contemporary art.

Guests can eat breakfast on the rooftop patio of San Michele while taking in the picturesque views of the sea and the town's rooftops. While the nearby streets beckon exploration of the town's cultural gems, the hotel's health centre provides a variety of soothing treatments.

The opulent lodgings in Polignano a Mare, with their views of the shore and elegant decor, extend an invitation to immerse oneself in a world of splendour and grandeur. Each of these luxurious resorts provides a special combination of individualised care, wellness options, and fine dining experiences that honour the local cuisine.

These prestigious brands in Polignano a Mare's opulent lodging, whether you decide to stay in a resort perched on the cliffs or a cave hotel with an Adriatic view, guarantee a memorable getaway that will leave you spellbound by the charm of Puglia's coastal beauty.

Ostuni

Ostuni is a lovely jewel tucked away in the centre of Puglia and is frequently referred to as the "White City" because of its sparkling whitewashed structures. This lovely town offers a variety of opulent lodgings that highlight the special charm and hospitality of the area. Its meandering lanes and magnificent views of the Adriatic Sea. In this part of this book where luxury meets the appeal of Puglia's rustic surroundings, we provide a curated list of some of the most illustrious names in opulent lodging.

La Sommità Relais & Chateaux

La Sommità Relais & Chateaux is a boutique hotel that exudes sophistication and charm. It is located in Ostuni's ancient district. The hotel is housed in a 16th-century structure and features well furnished rooms and suites with views of the nearby mediaeval buildings.

The elegant furnishings of La Sommità are enhanced by a cosy rooftop patio where visitors may unwind and take in panoramic views of Ostuni's rooftops and the Adriatic Sea. The hotel's Michelin-starred restaurant showcases the gastronomic diversity of the area by presenting inventive takes on classic Puglian fare.

La Sommità Relais & Chateaux offers a world of luxury and elegance for those looking for a private and exclusive hideaway in the heart of Ostuni's ancient centre.

Masseria Cervarolo

Masseria Cervarolo is an opulent country estate surrounded by ancient olive trees that exude tranquility and genuineness. The Masseria, which was formerly a fortified farmhouse, has undergone a meticulous restoration to highlight the natural charm of the area.

The Masseria Cervarolo's tastefully decorated rooms and suites offer a fusion of cosiness and rustic elegance, offering visitors a tranquil refuge to rest. A magnificent backdrop for rest and renewal is created by the outdoor pool and lush gardens at the Masseria.

The Masseria's restaurant focuses on farm-to-table eating and delivers delicious dishes produced with ingredients that are sourced locally, giving guests a true flavour of Puglia's culinary heritage.

Ostuni Palace Hotel

The beautiful 4-star Ostuni Palace Hotel, which is situated in the city's historic district, combines contemporary comfort with old-world elegance. The hotel is housed in a historic structure, and its furnishings, which include vaulted ceilings and artisanal accents, mirror the town's traditional architectural style.

The large, nicely decorated rooms offer guests a comfortable haven, and the rooftop terrace offers breathtaking panoramic views of the surrounding countryside and Ostuni's ancient rooftops.

The central position of the Ostuni Palace Hotel makes it the perfect starting point for exploring the charming ambience of Ostuni and its cultural riches.

The opulent lodgings in Ostuni provide a charming synthesis of old-world charm, modern luxury, and Puglian warmth. Each of these well-known brands in opulent housing offers a remarkable experience, inviting visitors to take in the beauty of Puglia's White City while luxuriating in top-notch amenities and attentive care.

These opulent lodging options in Ostuni promise an unforgettable escape that celebrates the beauty of Puglia's landscapes and the depth of its cultural heritage, whether you choose to stay in a centuries-old Masseria surrounded by olive groves or a boutique hotel inside the town's historic centre.

Fasano

A little-known jewel in the centre of Puglia is the lovely village of Fasano, which is nestled on the slopes of the Itria Valley. In the midst of centuries-old olive orchards and with sweeping views of the Adriatic Sea, Fasano provides a range of opulent lodgings that perfectly capture the spirit of calm luxury and polished elegance. You're invited to immerse yourself in the enchantment of this lesser-known Puglian paradise by showcasing a hand-picked list of some of the most prominent names in opulent lodging in Fasano.

Borgo Egnazia

Borgo Egnazia, one of the most well-known names in opulent lodging in Puglia, extends its grace and allure to the Fasano hills. This opulent resort resembles a typical Apulian village and is tucked away among olive orchards with views of the Adriatic Sea. It provides a seamless fusion of ancient architecture and contemporary amenities.

The rooms, suites, and private villas at Borgo Egnazia are artistically decorated with careful attention to every last detail, offering a haven of peace and tranquility. A luxurious spa, multiple swimming pools, and entry to an exclusive beach club are among the resort's attractions. The Adriatic Sea is also nearby.

Borgo Egnazia is a popular option for visitors looking for elegant elegance in Fasano because of its dedication to maintaining Puglia's rich cultural heritage and providing an unmatched guest experience.

Masseria San Domenico

Masseria San Domenico is a historic 5-star resort that typifies the grandeur of Puglian hospitality, perched on the seaside hills of Fasano. This historic watchtower, which dates to the fifteenth century, has been meticulously restored to offer a seamless fusion of old-world beauty and modern comfort.

Elegantly furnished, the Masseria San Domenico's rooms and suites have breathtaking views of the neighbouring olive orchards and the sea. The luxurious spa at the resort is a haven of tranquility where visitors may savour restorative treatments influenced by the local natural resources.

For those looking for an outstanding and opulent escape in Fasano, Masseria San Domenico is the ideal retreat thanks to the resort's private beach, championship golf course, and fine dining options.

Masseria Torre Coccaro

Masseria Torre Coccaro is an opulent country hideaway that radiates authenticity and peace. It is tucked away among centuries-old olive trees and conveniently located near the sea. The Masseria offers a charming setting for a chic getaway in the heart of Puglia with its whitewashed walls and historic stone elements.

A serene haven for guests to rest, Masseria Torre Coccaro's tastefully decorated rooms and suites offer the ideal fusion of rustic charm and contemporary luxury. The Masseria's extensive grounds, outdoor pool, and proximity to the sea provide a picturesque location for rest and renewal.

The restaurant at Masseria Torre Coccaro exhibits the flavours of Puglian cuisine and serves delicious dishes produced with products that are grown nearby. Masseria Torre Coccaro is the perfect accommodation option in Fasano for people looking for a quiet and genuine retreat.

Masseria Cimino

Masseria Cimino, a beautiful country estate that epitomises Puglia's pastoral charm, is tucked away among the olive-covered hills of Fasano. While providing contemporary conveniences and opulent amenities, the Masseria's antique architecture, with its stone walls and vaulted ceilings, transports visitors to a bygone age.

The Masseria Cimino's rooms and suites provide a tranquil and private getaway with lovely views of the surroundings. The outdoor pool and garden of the masseria provide a tranquil setting for relaxation and taking in Puglia's natural beauty.

Masseria Cimino offers a traditional Puglian experience that mixes elegance with rustic charm thanks to its friendly hospitality and dedication to protecting the area's cultural heritage.

The opulent lodging options in Fasano invite guests to discover the alluring allure of the Itria Valley and the splendour of Puglia's Adriatic coastline. With their top-notch amenities, spectacular vistas, and individualised treatment, each of these illustrious brands in opulent lodging offers a singular and remarkable experience.

Whether you select a boutique hotel in the heart of the town's historic district or an ancient Masseria nestled by olive orchards, these opulent lodging options in Fasano guarantee a magical vacation that honours the beauty of Puglia's landscapes and the depth of its cultural legacy.

Lecce

Due to its magnificent Baroque architecture, Lecce is frequently referred to as the "Florence of the South" and is a fascinating city rich in tradition. Travellers looking for upscale accommodations with first-rate service can find them in the centre of this creative treasure. In this part of this book, where elegance meets the alluring beauty of Puglia's cultural centre, we give a carefully curated list of some of the most illustrious brands in opulent lodging in Lecce.

Patria Palace Hotel

The Patria Palace Hotel is an opulent 5-star hotel that honours the grandeur and history of Lecce and is located in the city's old district. The hotel is housed in a 17th-century palace, and its rooms radiate a classic elegance with lavish furnishings and period-appropriate accents.

At Patria Palace, the tastefully decorated rooms and suites offer a harmonious fusion of traditional charm and contemporary luxury. The hotel's rooftop patio provides guests with sweeping views of Lecce's famous Baroque buildings and a relaxing environment.

A culinary trip that enthrals the senses is provided by the gourmet restaurant at Patria Palace, which provides outstanding regional cuisine that highlight the flavours of Puglia's culinary history. The Patria Palace Hotel guarantees an amazing stay in the centre of the city thanks to its strategic location and dedication to protecting Lecce's cultural heritage.

Risorgimento Resort

The exquisite 5-star Risorgimento Resort is a short distance from Lecce's central centre and flawlessly combines modern design with classic beauty. The hotel is housed in a 19th-century structure, and its interiors are decorated with contemporary art and opulent furnishings to create a posh atmosphere.

The Risorgimento Resort's rooms and suites provide a restful and fashionable escape, with many offering views of Lecce's ancient streets and landmarks. The hotel's wellness centre provides a haven of relaxation and well-being with a variety of pampering services.

The gourmet restaurant at the Risorgimento Resort features inventive takes on classic Puglian dishes, and its stylish rooftop bar provides a mesmerising backdrop for sipping cocktails and taking in views of Lecce's skyline.

La Fiermontina Urban Resort

La Fiermontina Urban Resort, a magnificent hideaway that seamlessly combines modern design with the city's cultural legacy, is located amidst lush gardens in the old district of Lecce. For discerning travellers, this meticulously renovated palace from the 17th century offers an intimate and unique experience.

The La Fiermontina's guest rooms and suites radiate a subtle elegance with their modern furnishings and decorative touches. The peaceful courtyard and outdoor pool area of the resort offer a pleasant haven for leisure.

A stay at La Fiermontina will immerse you in the artistic ambiance of Lecce and be enriched by the resort's dedication to exhibiting local art and culture.

Grand Hotel di Lecce

The Grand Hotel di Lecce is a five-star luxury hotel that combines traditional elegance with contemporary comfort. The hotel is housed in a building from the early 20th century, and its interiors are decorated with fine details and a charming blend of antique and modern furnishings.

The Grand Hotel di Lecce's rooms and suites have a warm, welcoming ambiance that makes them the perfect place for visitors to unwind. Lecce's old district is beautifully visible from the hotel's rooftop terrace, which makes for a magnificent environment for relaxation.

The restaurant of Grand Hotel di Lecce delivers delicious regional food that celebrates the flavours of Puglia and provides a great gastronomic experience.

Palazzo Persone Luxury Suites

The Palazzo Persone Luxury Suites is an intimate and upscale boutique hotel that perfectly encapsulates the aesthetic appeal of Lecce. It is tucked away in a historic structure in the centre of the city. The hotel's interiors perfectly blend traditional elements with cutting-edge style to produce a posh, elegant ambiance.

The elegantly decorated apartments of Palazzo Persone provide visitors with a secluded haven of luxury. The hotel's rooftop terrace offers enthralling views of Lecce's spectacular cityscape and is the perfect place to unwind and take in the beauty of the area.

Every visitor to Palazzo Persone receives a unique and customised experience because to the hotel's dedication to personalised service and attention to detail.

The opulent lodging options in Lecce encourage visitors to fully experience the aesthetic and cultural splendour of Puglia's "Florence of the South." Each of these well-known brands in opulent housing provides a distinctive and remarkable experience, fusing contemporary comfort with classic charm and unmatched service.

These lodging options in Lecce guarantee an enchanted vacation that honours the fascination of Puglia's cultural centre, whether you select a huge palace in the middle of the city or a small boutique hotel tucked away in old alleys.

Salento Peninsula

The Salento Peninsula, a picturesque area in Puglia's southernmost district, is well-known for its immaculate beaches, clean waters, and extensive cultural history. Travellers may experience a memorable escape amidst the grandeur of the Adriatic and Ionian Seas at this seaside paradise, which provides a variety of opulent lodgings that personify opulence and peace. Here, we'll provide a hand-picked list of some of the most renowned brands in opulent lodging on the Salento Peninsula, where sophistication meets the appeal of Puglia's southern jewel.

Furnirussi Tenuta

Furnirussi Tenuta is an opulent 5-star resort that provides a haven of leisure and well-being. It is surrounded by a natural grove of old olive trees. The resort's sleek, modern aesthetic blends seamlessly with the scenic surroundings of the Salento region.

The large rooms and suites at Furnirussi Tenuta have their own terraces or balconies with views of the resort's infinity pool or the olive fields nearby. A tranquil haven for relaxation, the resort's wellness centre offers a variety of luxurious treatments and therapies.

Furnirussi Tenuta's gourmet restaurant, which focuses on organic and locally sourced food, delivers mouthwatering meals that highlight the flavours of Puglia and takes customers on a gastronomic tour of the area's best ingredients.

Palazzo Daniele

The elegant boutique hotel palace Daniele is housed in a famous palace from the 19th century and expertly combines modern design with historical architecture. In the centre of the Salento Peninsula, in the village of Gagliano del Capo, the hotel offers a genuine and private experience.

The Palazzo Daniele's tastefully decorated rooms and suites combine contemporary conveniences with artistic touches to create a posh ambiance. Visitors can relax and take in the tranquility of the area in the hotel's garden and courtyard.

An educational and memorable visit on the Salento Peninsula is made possible by Palazzo Daniele's commitment to displaying modern art and cultural events.

The Salento Peninsula's opulent lodgings invite visitors to savour the tranquil beauty and cultural diversity of Puglia's southern jewel. Each of these prominent brands in opulent housing provides a distinctive and unforgettable experience, fusing modern comfort with the genuine charm of the locale.

Monopoli

Puglia's gorgeous seaside village of Monopoli is well known for its enchanting ancient town, magnificent beaches, and clear waters. A variety of opulent lodging options are available to those looking for sophisticated elegance and life-changing experiences within this exquisite setting. Here, you'll be provided with a curated list of some of the most illustrious names in opulent lodging in Monopoli.

Il Melograno

Il Melograno is a 5-star resort surrounded by centuries-old olive trees and vineyards that exudes old-world charm and classic elegance. The resort is housed in a 17th-century masseria, and its interiors have vaulted ceilings, stone walls, and magnificent antique furniture to create a posh atmosphere.

The luxuriously appointed rooms and suites at Il Melograno provide a calm getaway with views of the nearby gardens and countryside. The resort's verdant gardens, outdoor pool, and spa offer a tranquil haven for rest and renewal.

The gourmet restaurant at Il Melograno delivers mouthwatering Puglian cuisine made with fresh ingredients from the property's gardens and nearby farms, ensuring an authentic dining experience that honours the regional flavours.

Don Ferrante

The Don Ferrante - Dimore di Charme is an opulent boutique hotel that epitomises sophistication and exclusivity. It is perched atop the historic city walls with a view of the sea. This fortification from the tenth century has been lovingly refurbished to provide a private and opulent retreat in the middle of Monopoli's historic district.

The hotel's rooms and suites provide visitors a chic and private atmosphere with a blend of modern design features and vintage charm. The rooftop patio creates a magical setting for leisure by providing panoramic views of the Adriatic Sea and the town's charming streets.

Every visitor will have a unique and customised experience because of Don Ferrante's dedication to personalised service and attention to detail.

La Peschiera

La Peschiera - Resort & Spa is an opulent getaway with a view of the Adriatic Sea and is only a short distance from Monopoli's historic district. The resort's modern architecture seamlessly blends with the rocky coastline backdrop to produce a calming and opulent atmosphere.

La Peschiera provides a variety of tastefully furnished guestrooms, suites, and private villas, each with a patio or balcony and breath-taking ocean views. The resort's opulent spa offers a variety of rejuvenating treatments, and its fine-dining restaurant highlights the local cuisine.

La Peschiera in Monopoli ensures a wonderful seaside vacation with private beach access and attentive service.

Carlo V Hotel Spa & Resort

The Carlo V Hotel Spa & Resort is an opulent 5-star establishment that honours the town's maritime history and is tucked away within the ancient walls of Monopoli's old town and overlooking the sea. The hotel is housed in a stronghold from the sixteenth century, and its furnishings combine old-world charm with contemporary conveniences to provide a luxurious and exclusive refuge.

After discovering Monopoli's cultural treasures, guests can unwind in the Carlo V Hotel's tastefully appointed rooms and suites. The hotel's rooftop patio creates a lovely environment for relaxing with panoramic views of the Adriatic Sea and the town's picturesque roofs.

While the gourmet restaurant serves mouthwatering dishes that highlight the best components of Puglian cuisine, the spa at the Carlo V Hotel offers a variety of luxurious treatments.

The elegant lodgings in Monopoli encourage visitors to savour the allure and coastline splendour of Puglia's charming town. Each of these well-known brands in opulent lodging provides a distinctive and remarkable experience by fusing modern comfort with classic elegance and attentive service.

These opulent lodging options in Monopoli, whether you select a traditional Masseria surrounded by olive orchards or a boutique hotel located above the city walls, promise a charming vacation that honours the draw of Puglia's maritime splendour.

Alberobello

A UNESCO World Heritage site, Alberobello is a picturesque village in Puglia known for its distinctive trulli homes with conical roofs. Travellers looking for an unforgettable experience amidst classic architectural wonders will find a variety of exquisite hotels amidst this old town's alluring charm. In this part of the book, we provide a hand-picked list of some of the most renowned names in opulent lodging in Alberobello, where sophistication meets the attraction of Puglia's trulli-dotted village.

Grand Hotel La Chiusa di Chietri

Grand Hotel La Chiusa di Chietri is a luxury 4-star resort that provides a tranquil refuge in the Puglian countryside. It is surrounded by olive trees and is only a short drive from Alberobello's historic district. Rustic elegance is created by the harmonious blending of the resort's architecture and the traditional trulli dwellings.

La Chiusa di Chietri's guest rooms and suites radiate luxury and style while offering a tranquil getaway. The resort's outdoor pool is surrounded by beautiful grounds and provides a lovely environment for relaxation and taking in the scenery.

The restaurant at La Chiusa di Chietri delivers delicious dishes that highlight the flavours of Puglian cuisine and take customers on a gastronomic tour of the best ingredients from the area.

Trulli Resort Monte Pasubio

The opulent Trulli Resort Monte Pasubio is situated in the centre of Alberobello's trulli district, giving visitors access to the region's distinctive cone-shaped homes' timeless appeal. The trulli at the resort have undergone painstaking restoration, keeping its traditional features while adding contemporary conveniences.

The Trulli Resort Monte Pasubio's rooms and suites provide a genuine and individualised experience that fully immerses visitors in the heritage and culture of Alberobello. The resort's outside patio provides a special location to take in the trulli district's magnificence.

Trulli Resort Monte Pasubio provides an amazing stay in the centre of Alberobello's picturesque environment thanks to its strategic location and commitment to conserving the history of the trulli buildings.

Le Alcove

Le Alcove - Luxury Hotel is a magnificent boutique hotel that embraces the essence of classic architecture while offering contemporary sophistication. It is tucked away among the trulli dwellings. The hotel's trulli have been meticulously renovated and transformed into opulent rooms.

Le Alcove's apartments provide a posh and quiet atmosphere, and some even come with private outdoor hot tubs for an added touch of luxury. The hotel's patio has sweeping views of the trulli neighbourhood, making it a charming place to unwind and take in Alberobello's enchanted atmosphere.

Le Alcove's commitment to individualised service guarantees that visitors have a remarkable and customised experience in the centre of this distinctive village.

Tipico Resort

Tipico Resort is an opulent hotel that provides an immersive experience amid Alberobello's historic architecture. It is tucked away within a group of trulli homes. The trulli at the resort have undergone meticulous restoration, combining rustic charm with modern comfort.

In the trulli district's picturesque surroundings, the rooms and suites at Tipico Resort provide a serene haven. The resort's garden offers a tranquil setting to unwind and take in Alberobello's distinctive architecture.

Tipico Resort guarantees a unique experience while visiting this extraordinary village thanks to its commitment to presenting the trulli houses' authenticity and the warm hospitality of Puglia.

Travellers are invited to immerse themselves in Alberobello's opulent lodgings to experience the legendary trulli homes of Puglia's fairytale-like appeal. Each of these renowned brands in opulent housing provides a distinctive and remarkable experience, fusing modern luxury with the legendary appeal of Alberobello's classic architecture.

Whether you select a magnificent resort surrounded by the countryside or a lovingly renovated trullo situated within the village, these lodgings in Alberobello promise a magical getaway that honours the allure of Puglia's trulli-studded village.

Vieste

Seaside Opulence on the Gargano Coast is the name of one opulent hotel in Vieste.

The Gargano Peninsula's lovely seaside village of Vieste is renowned for its breathtaking cliffs, sandy beaches, and clean waters. A variety of opulent lodging options are available to those looking for an extraordinary experience in Puglia's beach paradise among this amazing natural beauty. In this part of this book, where refinement meets the attraction of the Gargano Coast, we give a hand-picked list of some of the most renowned names in opulent housing in Vieste.

Pizzomunno Vieste Palace Hotel

Pizzomunno Vieste Palace Hotel is an opulent 5-star resort perched on a rocky cliff overlooking the Adriatic Sea. It embodies coastal elegance and leisure. The hotel's architecture blends in perfectly with its natural surroundings, offering a tranquil atmosphere with easy access to the beach.

The Pizzomunno Vieste Palace Hotel's rooms and suites radiate comfort and elegance, with many providing spectacular sea views from private balconies or terraces. A peaceful place to unwind and take in the breathtaking seaside views is provided by the hotel's infinity pool and sun terrace.

The gourmet restaurant at Pizzomunno Vieste Palace Hotel delivers delightful meals influenced by the area's culinary tradition, giving visitors a taste of Puglia's most exquisite flavours.

Forte Hotel

The opulent Forte Hotel, a 4-star institution with direct access to the sea and a setting among olive trees, emanates tranquilly and exclusivity. The hotel's modern architecture blends seamlessly with the coastal scenery to produce a sophisticated, up-to-date ambience.

Many of the Forte Hotel's rooms and suites have balconies or terraces, providing a quiet and opulent hideaway. The hotel's outdoor pool area offers a tranquil haven for relaxation and enjoyment of the Gargano Coast's unspoiled beauty.

The restaurant at the Forte Hotel offers gourmet food that showcases Puglia's finest ingredients and takes diners on a tour of the area's culinary customs.

Hotel Pellegrino Palace

The opulent boutique hotel Pellegrino Palace Hotel is a short walk from Vieste's historic district and honours the town's maritime history. The hotel's furnishings, which combine modern design with vintage accents to create a timeless ambiance, are housed in a historic building.

The Pellegrino Palace Hotel's rooms and suites radiate luxury and comfort, with some offering views of Vieste's ancient streets. The rooftop terrace of the hotel offers expansive views of the city and the ocean, making it a compelling place to unwind and take in the natural beauty of the coast.

The restaurant at the Pellegrino Palace Hotel serves wonderful dishes that highlight the flavours of the region's culinary gems and give visitors a true sense of Puglia.

The opulent lodgings in Vieste encourage visitors to fully appreciate the coastline magnificence and cultural diversity of Puglia's Gargano Peninsula. Each of these renowned brands in opulent lodging provides a singular and remarkable experience, fusing modern comfort with the unmistakable attraction of Vieste's seaside beauty.

Torre Canne

The tranquil coastal community of Torre Canne in Puglia is well known for its white sands, azure waters, and natural hot springs. Travellers looking for an unforgettable experience by the sea can choose from a variety of opulent hotels in this lovely environment. Here, you'll get to know some of the most illustrious names in opulent lodging.

Hotel Canne Bianche_Lifestyle & Hotel

The exquisite 4-star Canne Bianche_Lifestyle Hotel is an embodiment of coastal calm and elegance, set within lush gardens with easy access to the beach. The resort's architecture integrates the surrounding environment to create a contemporary, sophisticated atmosphere with a hint of Mediterranean charm.

The Canne Bianche_Lifestyle Hotel's rooms and suites provide a calm haven, with many including private balconies or terraces with views of the grounds or the sea. The resort's outdoor pool and sun deck offer a tranquil place to unwind and take in the views of the coastline.

The restaurant at the Canne Bianche_Lifestyle Hotel delivers delicious Puglian and Mediterranean food using fresh, regional products to give customers a true taste of the area.

Exclusiveness and Privacy in Off-the-Beaten-Path Locations

Puglia is home to undiscovered hidden treasures where opulent hotels provide the utmost in seclusion and luxury. For those looking for a peaceful break from the noise and bustle of the outside world, certain isolated rural Masserie and villas tucked away among the olive orchards provide a tranquil haven.

You have the chance to detach from the outside world and reconnect with the genuineness of rural Puglia in these off-the-beaten-path locales. In these secret havens of luxury, indulge in private chef services, take advantage of one-on-one concierge support, and savour the peace and quiet of nature.

Unusual Encounters and Customised Services

Luxury hotels in Puglia go above and beyond to provide their visitors with unique experiences and personalised services. Personalised wine and olive oil tastings, private boat journeys to discover the nearby caves, and helicopter flights over the picturesque landscape are just a few examples of the personalised services offered.

The employees at opulent lodgings in Puglia take great satisfaction in making lifelong memories for their respected guests, whether it be planning romantic surprises for special occasions or designing uncommon cultural activities.

Important Advice for Luxurious Lodging

- Reserve Early

Puglia has a high demand for upscale lodging, especially in the summer and winter. To ensure your chosen choice, it is advised to make reservations well in advance.

- Dining Experiences
Enjoy fine dining at the opulent hotels' on-site restaurants, where experienced cooks create delightful meals using top-quality regional ingredients.

- Wellness and spa services
Puglia has many opulent lodging options with spas and health centres where you may indulge yourself to relaxing massages and treatments.

- Cultural Immersion
Don't pass up the chance to experience Puglia's rich heritage while indulging in luxury. Visit adjacent towns, indulge in regional celebrations, and engage in genuine activities that highlight the customs of the area.

The opulent hotels in Puglia provide a world of exclusivity, beauty, and customised experiences. Each lodging in this wonderful region promises an unmatched experience, from the beach retreats of Polignano a Mare and Monopoli to the trulli elegance in Alberobello and the off-the-beaten-path escapes. While travelling through this sun-drenched paradise, indulge in the greatest comforts and first-rate service while taking in the splendour of Puglia. Whether you're looking for a beach sanctuary or a rural hideaway, Puglia's opulent lodgings guarantee a once-in-a-lifetime experience that will leave you spellbound and itching to go back.

Best Places for Budget-Friendly Accommodation

Puglia, with its attractive landscapes and fascinating history, provides travellers looking for affordable amenities without sacrificing an authentic Italian experience with a variety of cost-effective accommodation options. This part of this guide will lead you to some of the best options for inexpensive lodging in Puglia, regardless of whether you're a backpacker seeking out the region's undiscovered gems, a family on a tight budget vacation, or a lone traveller hoping to fully experience the local culture.

Bari

Puglia's capital, Bari, is a bustling metropolis rich in tradition, culture, and coastline allure. Visitors to this fascinating city can choose from a variety of affordable lodging alternatives that provide convenience, comfort, and a taste of local hospitality without breaking the bank. Here is a list of some of the most reasonably priced and value-packed accommodations in Bari so that travellers on a tight budget may still have a great time exploring Puglia.

B&B La Muraglia.

Located in Bari's historic district, B&B La Muraglia is a comfortable and reasonably priced bed and breakfast that provides a warm and homely atmosphere. The B&B's attractively appointed rooms provide visitors who are discovering the city's cultural attractions a cosy and carefree stay.

The Basilica of San Nicola and the Castello Normanno-Svevo are just a couple of the famous Bari landmarks that are conveniently close to B&B La Muraglia thanks to its prime location. The friendly hospitality of the hosts gives the stay a personalised touch and gives visitors a sense of belonging to the neighbourhood.

Budget travellers looking for a special experience in the centre of Bari will find B&B La Muraglia to be a great choice thanks to its reasonable prices and convenient location.

Hotel Moderno

Hotel Moderno, a reasonably priced lodging choice close to Bari's main train station, makes a good starting point for exploring the city and the greater Puglia area. The hotel's rooms are cosy and well-appointed, providing all the facilities needed for a comfortable stay.

The Teatro Petruzzelli and the historic old town are two of the city's top attractions, and Hotel Moderno is ideally situated for visitors who want to sightsee and explore Bari's cultural landmarks.

For those travelling through or staying a few days in Bari, Hotel Moderno provides a sensible and cost-effective lodging option with its reasonable rates and handy location.

St. Nicholas Plaza

Saint Nicholas Plaza is a reasonably priced hotel that offers a comfortable stay for visitors looking for quick access to the city's business and recreational amenities. It is situated in the centre of Bari's commercial sector. After a day of visiting the city, guests can unwind in the hotel's functional though basic accommodations.

Visitors may easily explore Bari's shopping districts, dining options, and cultural attractions thanks to Saint Nicholas Plaza's strategic position. Just a short distance from the hotel are the famous Basilica of San Nicola and the busy Via Sparano.

Saint Nicholas Plaza is a cost-effective and practical lodging alternative in the centre of business in Bari for travellers on a tight budget.

Campus Hotel

Campus Hotel, a cost-effective lodging choice that welcomes both leisure and business travellers, is located close to Bari's university zone. The hotel's rooms are cosy and furnished with the necessities for a comfortable stay.

The Campus Hotel's location provides quick access to the university facilities in Bari as well as the city's historic district and coastal promenade. Visitors can stroll around the neighbourhoods in Bari that are favourable to students and take in the bustling ambiance of the city's pubs and cafes.

For travellers looking for inexpensive lodging with a hip ambiance, Campus Hotel is a great option because of its reasonable pricing and proximity to Bari's universities and cultural centres.

Travellers looking for accessible and comfortable places to stay in the centre of Puglia's capital city will find a great selection of economical options in Bari.

Lecce

Lecce, sometimes known as "Florence of the South" is a beautiful city in Puglia that is well-known for its extensive history, spectacular Baroque architecture, and thriving cultural life. Visitors to this enchanting city can choose from a variety of inexpensive lodging alternatives that provide ease, comfort, and a true sense of Lecce's charm without breaking the bank. Here, you'll see a list of some of the most reasonably priced and value-packed accommodations in Lecce, so that travellers on a tight budget can have a magical stay in the centre of this Baroque jewel.

B&B Palazzo Bernardini

Budget-friendly bed and breakfast B&B Palazzo Bernardini is housed in a historic structure in the heart of the old town of Lecce. The B&B's attractively appointed rooms provide visitors who are discovering the city's cultural attractions a cosy and comfortable place to stay.

The Porta Napoli and the Roman Amphitheatre are just a couple of the top attractions in Lecce that are conveniently close to B&B Palazzo Bernardini. The accommodating hosts provide a friendly and individualised experience that makes visitors feel as though they are a part of the neighbourhood.

B&B Palazzo Bernardini offers an authentic and private stay in the centre of Lecce with its reasonable rates and historic beauty.

Dimora dei Figuli

Dimora dei Figuli is a low-cost inn that immerses visitors in the region's architectural history and is housed in a typical Lecce townhouse. Travellers can stay in the guesthouse's cosy rooms, which are furnished with regional crafts and offer a distinctive and genuine experience.

The Piazza Sant'Oronzo and the Basilica di Santa Croce, as well as other cultural landmarks of Lecce, are conveniently close to Dimora dei Figuli. The courtyard of the guesthouse is a pleasant place to relax and take in the serene atmosphere.

For those on a tight budget looking for an authentic experience in the city, Dimora dei Figuli is a charming choice with its reasonable rates and immersion in Lecce's handmade traditions.

For visitors looking for a cosy and genuine stay in the centre of this Baroque jewel of Puglia, Lecce's modest lodgings provide a wide variety of affordable possibilities. These cost-effective hotels make a perfect base for your Puglian journey, whether you want to see the city's architectural wonders, indulge in local food, or just take in the lively environment.

Trani

Trani, a little port city on Puglia's Adriatic coast, is home to a fascinating past, beautiful architecture, and a scenic harbour. Trani offers a range of inexpensive lodging choices that give comfort, convenience, and a sense of the town's nautical attraction for visitors seeking an enthralling seaside experience without breaking the bank. Below are some hotels:

Hotel San Paolo al Convento

Budget-friendly Hotel San Paolo al Convento provides travellers looking for a peaceful retreat with a distinctive and tranquil location in a beautifully restored former convent. After discovering the town's cultural riches, guests can unwind in the hotel's attractively appointed rooms.

The stately Trani Cathedral and the famous harbour are just a short distance away from the Hotel San Paolo al Convento thanks to its convenient position in the heart of Trani. The courtyard and patio of the hotel offer tranquil spaces to unwind and take in the Mediterranean breeze.

Budget tourists looking for a taste of history when visiting Trani will find Hotel San Paolo al Convento to be a lovely choice thanks to its reasonable pricing and historic environment.

Hotel Regia Restaurant

The Hotel Regia Restaurant is a reasonably priced choice that offers contemporary comfort and close access to the sea and is situated just a few steps from Trani's lovely harbour. The hotel's rooms provide guests with a comfortable escape because they are cosy and furnished with necessary facilities.

Due to its prime position, Hotel Regia Restaurant offers quick access to the town's restaurants, landmarks, and Adriatic shore. The hotel's restaurant offers mouthwatering regional fare so visitors can experience Trani's culinary wonders.

For those on a tight budget looking for a beach getaway, Hotel Regia Restaurant provides a practical and comfortable option with its reasonable rates and close proximity to the shore.

B&B Porto

Budget-friendly B&B Porto is a guesthouse with spectacular sea views and a laid-back nautical vibe that is located beside Trani's harbour. The guesthouse's rooms are straightforward but cosy, offering visitors a peaceful haven while they explore the coastal town.

The old town's picturesque streets and Trani's seafront promenade are both conveniently close to B&B Porto's location. A perfect place to take in the seaside splendour and feel the sea breeze is on the guesthouse's terrace.

Budget-conscious visitors looking for a marine experience in Trani have a beautiful option with B&B Porto's reasonable rates and waterfront location.

Travellers looking for an authentic and comfortable stay by the Adriatic Sea can find a great selection of economical options in Trani's budget-friendly lodgings. These reasonably priced accommodations make a fantastic base for your Puglian journey.

Vieste

Puglia's Vieste, a charming village on the Gargano Peninsula, is home to breathtaking beaches, towering cliffs, and a rich cultural history. Vieste offers a range of inexpensive lodging choices for vacationers looking for a cost-effective beach trip that yet delivers comfort, convenience, and a true flavour of the Adriatic beauty. Here are some of the most reasonably priced and value-packed lodging options in Vieste:

Hotel Portonuovo

Hotel Portonuovo is a low-cost lodging option that provides guests seeking sun, sea, and relaxation with a coastal retreat that is only a few feet from Vieste's renowned Pizzomunno Beach. After a day of beachcombing, guests may return to the hotel's cosy rooms, which are furnished with all the necessities.

Visitors can fully take advantage of Hotel Portonuovo's proximity to the beach and the bustling town promenade. The breathtaking views of the sea and the well-known Pizzomunno Rock can be enjoyed from the hotel's sun deck.

For travellers on a tight budget looking for a coastal getaway in Vieste, Hotel Portonuovo presents a lovely option with its inexpensive rates and beachside location.

Hotel Scialara

Hotel Scialara is a reasonably priced alternative that offers comfort and convenience for those looking for a blend of town exploration and beach relaxation. It is situated only a short stroll from Vieste's historic centre. After a day of sightseeing, the hotel's rooms provide a peaceful escape with their natural light and warm decor.

The central position of the Hotel Scialara makes it simple to reach Vieste's lively squares, historical alleyways, and seaside vistas. The hotel's rooftop terrace offers a tranquil setting from which to take in the stunning seaside views.

For travellers on a tight budget, looking for a convenient place to stay in Vieste, Hotel Scialara is an appealing option thanks to its reasonable rates and convenient location.

Residence Maresol

Residence Maresol is a reasonably priced aparthotel that offers a home away from home for travellers wanting both independence and convenience. It is located close to Vieste's historic centre and only a short stroll from the beach. The well-equipped flats provide guests with a cosy and independent stay.

The Residence Maresol's position enables visitors to discover Vieste's historical sites, savour the regional cuisine, and spend peaceful days by the sea. The lawn of the aparthotel gives a peaceful haven for leisure.

For travellers on a tight budget looking for a flexible, self-catering stay in Vieste, Residence Maresol is a useful and comfortable option with its inexpensive rates and apartment-style living.

Hotel Sciali

The Hotel Sciali is a low-cost lodging choice that provides a family-friendly environment and necessary conveniences for a restful stay. It is close to Vieste's beaches and the old town. The hotel's rooms are straightforward but cosy, offering guests a tranquil haven.

The convenient location of Hotel Sciali makes it simple to visit Vieste's picturesque streets, bustling markets, and coastal promenade. The hotel's outdoor pool area is a cool place to relax and take in the Mediterranean sun.

Budget-conscious visitors looking for a laid-back and comfortable stay in Vieste will find Hotel Sciali to be an appealing alternative thanks to its reasonable pricing and family-friendly atmosphere.

For visitors seeking a cosy and genuine stay on the Gargano Peninsula, Vieste's inexpensive lodgings provide a wide variety of affordable possibilities.

Monopoli and Beyond

One of the numerous gems that embellish this lovely region of southern Italy is Monopoli, a charming beach town in Puglia. Beyond Monopoli, there are numerous charming towns and villages that each have their own distinctive charm and cultural history. It needn't be pricey for travellers on a tight budget to explore Puglia. For your Puglian vacation, this part of this book offers a list of budget-friendly lodging options in Monopoli and the surrounding communities.

B&B Casa Palmieri (Monopoli)

Budget-friendly guesthouse B&B Casa Palmieri, which is situated in the heart of Monopoli's historic district, offers a beautiful and cosy ambiance. The B&B's rooms are well furnished with a classic feel, providing visitors seeing the town's historic landmarks with a cosy haven.

The Charles V Castle, the Cathedral of Madonna della Madia, and the picturesque streets of Monopoli are all easily accessible from B&B Casa Palmieri's prime position. The B&B's hosts are renowned for their gracious hospitality, which makes for a pleasurable and genuine stay for visitors.

Budget-conscious travellers looking for an intimate experience in the centre of Monopoli have an appealing option with B&B Casa Palmieri's reasonable rates and convenient location.

Hotel Villa Rosa (Polignano a Mare)

Budget-friendly hotel Hotel Villa Rosa is situated in the charming village of Polignano a Mare, just a short drive from Monopoli. Travellers will enjoy a comfortable and well-appointed stay in the hotel's rooms.

The historical centre, Lama Monachile Beach, and Polignano a Mare's breathtaking cliffs are all conveniently close to Hotel Villa Rosa. The Adriatic Sea and the charming town are visible from the hotel's rooftop patio in all their magnificence.

Hotel Villa Rosa is a great choice for those on a tight budget looking for a tranquil beach vacation outside of Monopoli because of its reasonable prices and coastal beauty.

Masseria Il Frantoio (Ostuni)

Affordably priced agriturismo Masseria Il Frantoio is close to Ostuni and offers a genuine one-of-a-kind experience. This adorable property provides a look into Puglia's agricultural traditions and rustic elegance.

The comfortable, rural-themed rooms at Masseria Il Frantoio offer visitors a tranquil refuge. Olive orchards and gardens at the agriturismo provide a tranquil location for relaxing and taking in the countryside.

For travellers on a tight budget looking for a rural getaway, Masseria Il Frantoio offers a genuine and immersive choice with its reasonable pricing and agriturismo atmosphere.

The fascinating tour through Puglia's treasures doesn't end in Monopoli. As you travel further, you'll discover a variety of inexpensive lodging options in nearby towns and villages, each with its own special charm.

Alberobello

Puglia's enchanting hamlet of Alberobello, a UNESCO World Heritage Site, is well-known for its distinctive trulli houses, classic cone-shaped homes that dot the countryside. Alberobello has a range of inexpensive lodging alternatives for visitors. Below are some options:

Trulli and Puglia Resort

The affordable guesthouse Trulli and Puglia Resort is situated in the centre of Alberobello's trulli neighbourhood and provides a distinctive and genuine stay in the middle of the typical cone-shaped homes. The guesthouse's rooms are tucked away inside the trulli, giving visitors a singular experience.

Alberobello's famous trulli and ancient sites are easily accessible from Trulli and Puglia Resort due to its strategic location. The proprietors of the hostel are renowned for their cordial hospitality and insightful explanations of the customs and culture of the area.

For those on a tight budget looking for a genuine place to stay in Alberobello, Trulli and Puglia Resort presents a distinctive and endearing option with its reasonable rates and trulli immersion.

Trulli Family

Trulli Family is a reasonably priced bed & breakfast that offers guests looking for a taste of Puglian hospitality a warm and welcoming ambiance in the heart of Alberobello's trulli neighbourhood. The trulli that house the B&B's rooms give them a rustic and attractive atmosphere.

The Trulli Family's position makes it simple to reach Alberobello's charming streets and the two-story trullo known as the Trullo Sovrano, which doubles as a historical landmark and museum. The innkeepers are renowned for providing a friendly welcome and punctual service.

For those on a tight budget looking for an immersive stay in Alberobello, Trulli Family provides a lovely and real option with its reasonable pricing and trulli authenticity.

Trulli Holiday Resort

Trulli Holiday Resort is a reasonably priced aparthotel that offers a home away from home for travellers wanting both freedom and convenience, and is situated not far from Alberobello's trulli region. The well-equipped flats provide guests with a cosy and independent stay.

The Trulli houses and historical sites of Alberobello are conveniently close to Trulli Holiday Resort. The garden and outdoor pool area of the aparthotel offer a tranquil atmosphere for unwinding.

Budget-conscious visitors looking for a flexible, self-catering stay in Alberobello have an affordable option with Trulli Holiday Resort's reasonable rates and apartment-style living.

For visitors seeking a cosy and genuine stay amidst the alluring trulli cottages, Alberobello's inexpensive lodgings provide a great range of affordable choices.

Locorotondo

The scenic hilltop town of Locorotondo in Puglia is well known for its concentric white-washed buildings and charming lanes. One of Locorotondo's budget-friendly options will be discussed below:

B&B Lamie

B&B Lamie, a reasonably priced bed and breakfast outside the historic district of Locorotondo, provides a tranquil and quiet haven for tourists looking for a rural vacation. The B&B's rooms are inviting and furnished with necessary conveniences, offering visitors a peaceful respite.

The setting of B&B Lamie enables visitors to take in the peace of the Valle d'Itria while still being close to the allure of Locorotondo. The yard and outdoor spaces of the B&B provide a tranquil location for relaxation.

Budget-conscious visitors looking for a rural getaway close to Locorotondo will find B&B Lamie to be a pleasant choice thanks to its reasonable rates and charming rural setting.

Grottaglie

In the Puglian province of Taranto, the picturesque town of Grottaglie is well known for its long history of ceramics manufacturing. Grottaglie provides a range of inexpensive lodging options for those looking for a genuine and affordable experience in this creative town. They include:

B&B Casa delle Ceramiche

The B&B Casa delle Ceramiche is a reasonably priced inn that provides a distinctive and artistic stay among the town's pottery workshops. It is situated within Grottaglie's historic centre. Ceramic artworks are used to decorate the guesthouse's rooms, giving visitors a full sense of Grottaglie's craftsmanship.

The Church of San Francesco d'Assisi, the impressive Castle Episcopio, and the ceramics district of Grottaglie are all conveniently located near B&B Casa delle Ceramiche. The proprietors of the inn are renowned for their cordial hospitality and love of pottery.

Budget-conscious visitors looking for an immersive stay in Grottaglie have a unique and unforgettable alternative with B&B Casa delle Ceramiche's reasonable pricing and artistic environment.

B&B Il Furente

Budget-friendly B&B Il Furente is a bed and breakfast that offers guests looking for a taste of Puglian hospitality a warm and welcoming environment in one of Grottaglie's picturesque alleys. The B&B's rooms are cosy and beautifully equipped, providing visitors with a tranquil refuge.

The pottery studios of Grottaglie, the Baroque Church of Santissima Croce, and the Archaeological Park of Mura Messapiche are all conveniently close to B&B Il Furente. The B&B's hosts are renowned for their first-rate hospitality and local expertise.

Budget-conscious travellers looking for an intimate stay in the centre of Grottaglie have a charming and practical option in B&B Il Furente, thanks to its reasonable prices and handy location.

Coastal Camping and Glamping

Puglia offers a variety of camping and glamping alternatives along its unspoiled coastline for nature enthusiasts and budget vacationers looking for a seaside adventure. Glamping locations offer a taste of luxury in the great outdoors, and coastal camping areas offer an economical opportunity to appreciate the area's natural splendour.

Imagine spending your days discovering secluded coves and stunning beaches while drifting off to sleep under a starlit sky, waking up to the sound of crashing waves. You may make priceless moments in the midst of nature in Puglia by glamping and camping along the coast.

Crucial Advice for Finding Budget-Friendly Accommodation

- Off-Peak Travel
To take advantage of lower lodging costs, visit Puglia in the shoulder seasons or off-peak months.

- Local markets and trattorias
Eat for a reasonable price in neighbourhood markets and trattorias to experience true Puglian cuisine.

- Public Transportation

Take advantage of Puglia's economical public transportation choices, like the buses and trains that run between villages and cities.

- Shared Housing
To cut down on meal costs, look for lodgings that provide shared amenities like public kitchens.

- Reserve Early
Although there are affordable options, it's important to book in early to lock in the best deals, especially during the busiest travel times.

CHAPTER 5

Puglia's Culinary Delights

Southern Italy's Puglia, commonly referred to as Apulia, is renowned for its extensive culinary history. You will come across a wide variety of delectable foods as you travel across Puglia, reflecting the history, culture, and natural wealth of the area in your meals. Fresh fish, savoury pasta, delicious olive oil, and mouth watering pastries are just a few of Puglia's culinary delights, which celebrate the region's fertile soil and its inhabitants' inventiveness

Food in Puglia

Olive Oil

Puglia is one among Italy's top producers of this "liquid gold," and it is the foundation of Puglian cuisine. Nearly every dish in the local cuisine benefits from the fruity, extra virgin olive oil produced by the olive groves that dot the region.

Visitors can tour the several olive oil mills (frantoi) in the area where the traditional method of cold pressing olives is still used. A simple yet delicious experience that reflects the spirit of Puglia is to sprinkle some of this aromatic oil over some freshly made bread or a platter of veggies.

Orecchiette and Puglian Pasta

Orecchiette, a little, ear-shaped pasta that is a regional delicacy, is identified with Puglia. Orecchiette, which are traditionally formed by hand, are frequently eaten with a variety of sauces, such as the traditional "cime di rapa" (turnip greens), "ragù," or "pomodoro fresco."

Puglia has a wide variety of pasta variants in addition to orecchiette, each with a unique shape and use. Every type of pasta, from cavatelli and troccoli to strascinati and fidelini, has a distinctive texture that blends well with various components and sauces.

Seafood Extravaganza

The extensive coastline of Puglia and its proximity to the Adriatic and Ionian Seas guarantee a steady supply of fresh seafood for local cuisine. The "frutti di mare" (sea fruits) are an essential component of Puglian cuisine.

The meals "burrata di mare" (sea bream), "calamari ripieni" (stuffed squid), "seppie al nero" (cuttlefish in squid ink sauce), and "orata al forno" (oven-baked sea bream) are also common seafood dishes. The flavours are straightforward but lively, enabling the seafood's inherent flavour to stand out.

Street Food

The street food scene in Puglia is a culinary treat. A small, fried pastry filled with tomato, mozzarella, and occasionally other ingredients is known as a "panzerotto" and is a favourite snack. It is a favourite food eaten during festivals and gatherings held outside.

The "taralli," which are savoury, crunchy biscuits in the shape of rings, are another traditional street dish. Taralli are excellent for snacking or serving with a glass of wine and available in a variety of flavours like fennel, black pepper, or olive oil.

Breads and Focaccia

Some of Italy's most well-known bread variations originate in Puglia. A light flatbread called "focaccia barese" with a lot of olive oil is frequently topped with cherry tomatoes, olives, and oregano. It is frequently eaten for breakfast or as an appetiser.

Another distinctive bread from Puglia is called "puccia"; it resembles a sandwich roll and is usually filled with a variety of ingredients, including local cheeses, cured meats, and vegetables.

Dolci

Without indulging in some of Puglia's mouthwatering desserts, no gastronomic tour of the region would be complete. Small pastry shells called "pasticciotti," which are filled with custard or fruit jam, are a favourite among both locals and tourists in the area.

A favourite treat during Christmas and other festive events, "cartellate" are thin, fried pastry ribbons that are drizzled with honey or vincotto (cooked wine) and topped with almonds.

Cheese

Puglia has a delicious selection of cheeses made from both cow's milk and sheep's milk, making it a cheese lover's paradise. The rich, creamy "burrata" cheese is one of the most well-known in the area. Stracciatella, or shredded mozzarella drenched in cream, is added to a mozzarella pouch to create this exquisite cheese. A must-try treat, the luscious, creamy centre pours forth when the cake is cut open.

Another well-known cheese called "Caciocavallo" is distinguished by its unusual shape, which is called "cavallo" in Italian and resembles a saddle for a horse. When used in classic dishes like "orecchiette al sugo di caciocavallo," pasta topped with a creamy caciocavallo cheese sauce, this semi-hard cheese is frequently paired with crusty bread.

Vegetables and Legumes

Puglia's agricultural terrain is also evident in the variety of vegetables and legumes it produces. A typical and filling Puglian delicacy is "fave e cicorie," a meal made from fava beans and wild chicory. Fava beans' earthy flavours blend well with chicory's somewhat bitter flavour to provide a filling and nutrient-rich dish.

A creamy fava bean puree known as "puré di fave" is frequently offered as a side dish or as a spread on crostini. It displays the straightforwardness of Puglian cuisine, letting the pure flavours of the ingredients stand out.

Almond-based Pastries

Due to the Arab influence that existed in the area for centuries, Puglia is also well known for its almond-based pastries. Both locals and tourists adore "Pasticciotto Leccese," a delectable pastry filled with custard or jam and frequently flavoured with almond essence.

The "pasta di mandorla," small almond cakes with a delicate crumbly texture and frequently topped with a whole almond, are another treat made with almonds. These delectable treats are the ideal treat to enjoy after dinner or with an afternoon espresso.

Farm-to-Table Dining

Visitors can learn more about the idea of "agriturismi" in Puglia for a genuinely authentic gastronomic experience. Agriturismi are operating farms that also provide lodging and traditional cuisine created using materials grown on the property.

Guests can enjoy a farm-to-table dining experience where they can sample food made with just gathered fruits, vegetables, and meats while being surrounded by the rural beauty of Puglia.

Culinary Tours and Cooking Classes

Cooking workshops and food excursions are offered all throughout the region for foodies keen to learn more about Puglian cuisine. Local chefs and home cooks provide a hands-on introduction to the art of Puglian food by sharing their family recipes, cooking methods, and the tales behind each dish.

Visitors can learn about the production methods and sample the best goods the area has to offer on culinary tours that take them to bustling food markets, olive oil mills, and cheese dairies.

The culinary delights of Puglia are a tapestry of tastes, history, and culture that entice tourists to partake in a gourmet adventure unlike any other. Every dish served in Puglia, from the straightforward farm-to-table fare to the intricate seafood extravaganzas, expresses the region's uniqueness and its profound relationship to the land and the sea.

As you continue to discover Puglia, savour the region's many delicious flavours, immerse yourself in its rich culinary history, and make lasting memories among Puglia's alluring landscapes.

Culinary Districts and Food Courts

Puglia has witnessed a growing trend in the emergence of lively food courts and culinary districts that highlight the region's varied and mouth watering cuisine in recent years. These culinary hotspots are evidence of Puglia's rich culinary heritage and offer locals and guests a wonderful opportunity to experience the local flavours. These food courts and districts provide a wide variety of Puglian delicacies.

Fasanolandia

Fasanolandia, famous for its theme park and safari zoo, has a food court that offers something for everyone's palate. In the midst of the park's excitement, families and guests of all ages can indulge in a great gastronomic experience.

Food options in Fasanolandia's food court range from traditional Puglian meals like "orecchiette con le cime di rapa" to cosmopolitan fare, catering to a variety of tastes. It's the ideal place to get a quick snack before continuing the journey or to enjoy a leisurely meal to recover from a day of exploring.

Foggia Street Food Scene

The alleys of Foggia are lined with food trucks and stalls selling a tantalising array of regional specialties, creating a vibrant street food scene. Foggia's street food sellers satisfy all appetites with anything from classic "panzerotti" and "olive ascolane" (stuffed olives) to creative sweet and savoury crepes.

The bustling ambiance and the aroma of freshly prepared foods offer a tantalising culinary experience that entices visitors to taste the city's wide variety of flavours.

Gallipoli Fish Market

In addition to being a place to purchase fresh seafood, Gallipoli's fish market is also a popular dining destination where guests can sample some of Puglia's best seafood delicacies. The lively atmosphere of the market, filled with the cries of fishermen and the hues of the sea's wealth, creates the ideal setting for an actual culinary trip.

A wide variety of seafood specialties are available at neighbourhood restaurants near the fish market, including "scampi al guazzetto" (langoustines in a tomato and wine sauce) and "branzino al sale" (sea bass baked in salt). It exhibits the coastal gems of the area and is a seafood lover's heaven.

The food markets and culinary districts in Puglia are evidence of the inventiveness and wealth of the local cuisine. These culinary hotspots offer a variety of culinary experiences, catering to both traditionalists and those looking for new gastronomic excursions.

Elegant Dining

Puglia's culinary scene is not only bursting with regional specialties, but it also boasts a number of opulent eateries that cater to picky diners and take dining to a whole new level of elegance. These restaurants create a gourmet experience that is both memorable and decadent by combining the finest products from the area with artistic presentation and first-rate service. Puglia's upscale eateries, which range from seaside fine dining to charming countryside settings, entice visitors to experience the essence of the region's culinary creativity in chic and sumptuous settings.

Cielo Restaurant, Ostuni

A culinary delicacy with a coveted Michelin star can be found in Ostuni's mediaeval centre at Cielo Restaurant. This upscale dining establishment, run by a competent chef, highlights the finest of Puglian food with a modern touch.

Cielo Restaurant serves delicious cuisine that tempt the palate with an emphasis on fresh and locally sourced ingredients. Each meal is a work of art that honours the region's culinary tradition, from handcrafted pastas to creative desserts to freshly caught fish.

Grotta Palazzese Restaurant , Polignano a Mare

The picturesque coastal village of Polignano a Mare is home to the unique dining establishment Grotta Palazzese. This opulent restaurant offers a romantic and sophisticated environment as it is located inside a natural sea cave with views of the Adriatic Sea.

A wide variety of superb wines are available to accompany the gourmet menu's mouthwatering seafood dishes. The allure of this special dining location is enhanced by the natural beauty of the cave and the sound of waves lazily lapping against the rocks.

Masseria Il Frantoio Restaurant, Ostuni

Masseria Il Frantoio is a stunning masseria (farmhouse) with a posh restaurant located in the Apulian countryside close to Ostuni. The restaurant offers a tranquil and attractive atmosphere for a good dining experience since it is surrounded by olive gardens and historic olive trees.

The dishes served at Masseria II Frantoio highlight the regional flavours of Puglia and feature organic and locally sourced seasonal ingredients. The culinary competence of the chef and the genuineness of Puglian cuisine are evident in the inventiveness and finesse with which the dishes are produced.

Due Camini, Savelletri di Fasano

Due Camini is a renowned fine dining establishment that skillfully combines Puglian traditions with outside influences. It is situated inside the lovely Borgo Egnazia resort near Savelletri di Fasano. The name of the restaurant, which translates to "Two Chimneys," honours the two sizable fireplaces that provide a cosy and welcoming atmosphere.

Due Camini's culinary creations are a blend of flavours that use the best regional products and cutting-edge cooking methods. The wine selection enhances the eating experience by showing the greatest Italian and Puglian wines to go with the cuisine.

Masseria Torre Coccaro, Savelletri di Fasano

Not only is Masseria Torre Coccaro an opulent five-star resort, but it also houses a superb fine-dining establishment. The restaurant offers a stunning backdrop for an exceptional dining experience because it is situated between centuries-old olive orchards and looks out into the Adriatic Sea.

With a focus on organic and locally sourced ingredients, the culinary staff at Masseria Torre Coccaro creates a menu that highlights the finest of Puglian and Mediterranean cuisine. Visitors can savour regionally inspired delicacies like "pollo arrosto" (roasted chicken) flavoured with fragrant herbs from the Masseria's gardens and "cavatelli" with fresh tomato and "burrata."

La Sommità Relais & Chateaux, Ostuni

It is a charming boutique hotel in Ostuni and a gastronomic haven for food enthusiasts. A memorable eating experience is made possible by the restaurant's exquisite decor and patio that overlooks the town.

A symphony of flavours, featuring the best of Puglian and Italian traditions with a modern twist, can be found in the cuisine at La Sommità Relais & Chateaux. A memorable gastronomic experience is guaranteed by dishes like "risotto ai frutti di mare" (seafood risotto) and "agnello al melograno" (lamb with pomegranate), which highlight the originality and competence of the culinary crew.

The elegant settings and superb gastronomic artistry of Puglia's fine dining establishments are a monument to the region's culinary superiority. These gastronomic gems offer a variety of experiences that appeal to a wide range of tastes and inclinations, from picturesque villages and beachside paradises to historic masserie and seaside caverns.

Puglian Wine

Apulia, commonly known as Puglia, is a region with enchanted and varied landscapes, and this includes its wine legacy. Puglia is a wine lover's delight, known for its sun-drenched vineyards, age-old winemaking customs, and a wide variety of indigenous grape varietals. This guide to Puglian wine will introduce you to the region's oenological gems, historical winemaking techniques, and the magnificent wines that have been lauded by connoisseurs and treasured by locals for decades as you start your journey through the vineyards.

Ancient Winemaking Customs

The Greeks and Romans were the first to cultivate vines in this lush country, giving Puglia its long tradition of wine production. You'll see the ongoing presence of centuries-old winemaking practises that have been passed down through the generations as you tour the region's wineries.

You can observe the use of conventional winemaking methods and "palmenti," enormous stone vats where grapes are manually crushed, when you visit family-owned wineries. These techniques not only emphasise the cultural past of the area but also provide the wines a unique feeling of terroir and personality.

Native Grape Varieties

The wide variety of native grape varietals used to make Puglian wine is among its most alluring features. From the powerful "Primitivo" and "Negroamaro" to the refined "Nero di Troia" and "Susumaniello," Puglia's vineyards are a hidden gem of distinctive flavours just waiting to be discovered.

These regional grapes are used by vintners to create wines that capture the spirit of the area. You will be able to sample velvety reds, crisp whites, and effervescent rosés, each of which highlights a different aspect of Puglian terroir.

IGT, DOC, and DOCG

Several prestigious wine categories that guarantee the quality and provenance of its wines are found in Puglia. While Denominazione di Origine Controllata (DOC) and Denominazione di Origine Controllata e Garantita (DOCG) designate wines from specific regions and uphold severe standards, Indicazione

Geografica Tipica (IGT) includes wines that highlight the geographical features.

The DOC and DOCG marks on wine labels are guarantees that the wine was made with specific grape varietals, according to established winemaking procedures, and aged according to set standards. These awards demonstrate Puglia's dedication to creating great wines that pay homage to the region's winemaking history.

Salento

The Salento peninsula in Puglia stands out as a refuge for wine lovers, where grapes flourish in the warmth of the Mediterranean and the sea winds. The "Primitivo" and "Negroamaro" wines from the Salento area are well-known across the world for their robust flavours and silky textures.

Particularly the "Primitivo di Manduria," a red wine prized for its intense colour and aromas of dark fruits and spice, is famous across the world. You'll have the chance to sample these powerful and alluring wines while touring Salento's wineries and taking in the stunning vineyard vistas.

Itria Valley

The Itria Valley, well-known for its distinctive trulli homes, is also a place of exquisite viniculture. The "Locorotondo" and "Martina Franca" wines, both made from the "Verdeca" and "Bianco d'Alessano" grapes, may be found here.

A light white wine with flowery and citrus aromas that is named after the lovely village of "Locorotondo" and is ideal for drinking on a warm day. Contrarily, "Martina Franca" is a dry white wine with a characteristic minerality that goes excellently with regional seafood meals.

Castel del Monte

Without stopping in the Castel del Monte region, famous for its majestic octagonal castle and exceptional wines, no tour of Puglian wine would be complete. This region is dominated by the "Nero di Troia" grape, which yields powerful reds with hints of black cherries, licorice, and spices.

The wines produced by Castel del Monte, such as "Castel del Monte Nero di Troia Riserva," are a testament to the area's winemaking prowess and its capacity to create sophisticated vintages that stand up to some of the most prominent Italian labels.

Puglian Rosé

Rosé enthusiasts will be lured to the wonderful Puglian rosés since they offer a rainbow of hues and flavours. Puglian rosés, produced from several local grape varietals, come in a variety of colours, from soft salmon to vivid coral.

The wild strawberries, cherries, and hints of Mediterranean herbs that these light wines emit make them the ideal match for Puglia's warm environment and delicious cuisine.

Wine Festivals and Celebrations

All throughout the year, festivals and activities honouring the region's winemaking history are held to honour Puglia's wine culture. These events provide a singular chance to become immersed in Puglia's vinicultural traditions, from the "Cantine Aperte" (Open Wineries) celebration in May, where wineries open their doors to visitors, to the "Festival della Valle d'Itria" in Martina Franca, where wine is paired with music and performances.

Food and Wine Pairing

The unique culinary environment of Puglia makes for the perfect setting for experiments with food and wine pairing. There is a perfect wine to go with any dish, whether it be traditional fare like "orecchiette" with turnip greens or seafood specialties like "polpo alla pignata" (octopus stew).

Local winemakers and sommeliers are skilled at recommending the perfect wine to go with your dishes, providing a seamless blending of flavours that raises your dining experience to new heights.

Sustainable Winemaking

The terrain and the region's natural resources are revered greatly by Puglia's winemakers. Many vineyards use sustainable and organic winemaking techniques to grow grapes with little interference and little negative impact on the environment.

In addition to producing excellent wines, these eco-friendly initiatives help protect the stunning landscapes of the area and guarantee that future generations can continue to enjoy the wealth of Puglian wine.

Wine Tourism

Puglia provides a wine tourism experience unlike any other for connoisseurs of the beverage. Guided vineyard tours are available for wine enthusiasts, during which knowledgeable winemakers impart their expertise and passion for winemaking. Visitors can learn about the production of local grape types and the area's sustainable agricultural techniques by strolling around the lush vineyards.

Visits to wineries allow tourists to experience the winemaking process firsthand, from the pressing of grapes to the fermentation and oak barrel ageing processes. An intimate look into the creativity that goes into creating superb Puglian wines is provided via the immersive experience.

Wine with Olive Oil

Along with its wines, Puglia is well known for its premium olive oil. In Puglian cooking, wine and olive oil work well together because they enhance a variety of dishes.

A fascinating component of Puglian cuisine is visiting olive trees and learning about how olive oil is made. As many vineyards also produce their own extra virgin olive oil, guests can take a sensory tour that honours the two most prized agricultural commodities in the area.

Wine Festivals

In Puglia, the grape harvest is a big occasion that is marked by raucous festivities and festivals called "sagre." These celebrations honour the completion of a year's worth of laborious work in the vineyards and give locals and tourists alike the chance to partake in the fun.

During the "sagre," guests can savour freshly harvested grapes, dance to folk music, and sip a variety of Puglian wines. It's the perfect time to immerse yourself in Puglia's thriving wine culture because of the upbeat attitude, which is contagious.

Wine Trails

Numerous wine paths weave through gorgeous scenery and ancient towns in Puglia. These carefully chosen routes take visitors to the most prestigious wineries and scenic vineyards, each with its own special terroir and allure.

These wine trails, such as the "Strada del Vino e dell'Olio Castel del Monte" and the "Wine Road of the Ionian Coast," highlight the region's vinicultural diversity and let visitors design unique wine-tasting itineraries.

Wine and Art

Wine and art have a long history of coexisting in Puglia, where many vineyards see art as an essential component of their brand. The distinction between the cultural and viticultural spheres is muddled by the presence on the grounds of many wineries of modern art exhibitions, sculptures, and installations.

When visiting these wineries, tourists may enjoy wine and art side by side, creating an immersive experience that appeals to the palate and the senses.

Puglia's Dessert Wines

Puglia is renowned for both its decadent dessert wines and its dry wines. A sweet wine called "Primitivo Dolce Naturale," produced from the

"Primitivo" grape, seduces with its exquisite aromas of ripe fruit and spices.

When paired with local treats like "cartellate," "pasticciotti," and "zeppole di San Giuseppe," these dessert wines make for a pleasant end to a Puglian meal.

Wine Auctions

Wine auctions give collectors looking for the best Puglian wines a way to purchase expensive and uncommon bottles. Collectors and wine enthusiasts can place bids at events held by auction houses in Puglia on limited-edition vintages and recognisable labels.

Visitors can purchase remarkable bottles that represent the best representations of Puglian terroir and winemaking craftsmanship by taking part in a wine auction.

The Art of Wine Tasting

Wine tastings in Puglia go beyond a few sips and invite visitors on a sensory adventure. Visitors are taught how to distinguish the subtleties of fragrance, flavour, and texture by skilled sommeliers as they are guided through the complexities of wine tasting.

Wine lovers can better appreciate the complexity of Puglian wines and forge stronger relationships to the region's vinicultural legacy with the help of their newly acquired knowledge.

The symphony of tradition, terroir, and taste that is Puglia's wine culture beckons tourists to discover the enchanted vineyards and savour the soulful wines produced by centuries-old customs.

You'll come to appreciate the allure of Puglian wine as you travel through the region's vineyards, take part in wine festivals, and savour delicious food and wine pairings. This is an encounter that will live on in your palate and heart as a treasured memory for years to come. Raise a glass to Puglia's viticultural marvels and toast to the joy of wine, the region's elixir.

Puglia's Bar Scene

The lively and vivacious bar culture in Puglia is a reflection of the area's rich cultural heritage and sociable way of life. Bars are an essential part of the Puglian way of life, providing more than simply a place to relax with a drink. This is true of both the busy city streets and the charming coastal villages. The art of "passeggiata," the custom of "aperitivo," and the warmth of Puglian hospitality are all revealed as you dig into the region's pub culture, weaving a tapestry of amazing experiences.

The Passeggiata

The "passeggiata" is a beloved tradition that unites the community in Puglia each evening. Locals and visitors alike go to the streets as the sun sets to stroll casually around the promenades and plazas. It's a time for mingling, catching up with loved ones, and taking in the cool evening breeze.

In this endearing custom, bars serve a crucial role as meeting places where friends assemble to clink drinks and swap tales. Participating in the "passeggiata" provides a window into the centre of Puglia's social life, whether you're in a bustling city like Bari or a charming village like Polignano a Mare.

Aperitivo

Aperitivo is a crucial component of Puglian pub culture and a must-do activity. Aperitivo is a pre-dinner tradition that is typically held between late afternoon and early evening. During this time, guests can have a drink and a delicious selection of appetisers.

The "spuntini" that Puglia's pubs serve up are remarkable, ranging from cheese, olives, and bruschetta to regional specialties like "taralli" and "friselle." Enjoy your aperitivo while unwinding and enjoying the local flavours by pairing it with a crisp glass of Puglian wine or an old-fashioned "Aperol Spritz."

Caffè Culture

Puglian life is permeated by a strong coffee culture. Puglia has a long history with coffee, and the "caffè" plays a significant role in daily life. A cup of coffee in Puglia is an artistic creation, whether it is consumed in the morning, following a meal, or during a little break.

As you savour the tastes and scents of Puglian coffee, order a "caffè macchiato" (espresso with a dash of milk) or a "caffè leccese" (espresso with almond milk). Each sip is an indulgent moment thanks to the baristas' talent in creating the ideal cup, which enhances the pleasure.

The Bari Vecchia Experience

Traditional "osterie" and "friggitorie," which can be found in Bari Vecchia, the city's historic centre, give the bar scene there a distinct appeal. These eateries offer a delicious selection of regional street food, such as "pasticciotti" (sweet pastries), "sgagliozze" (fried polenta), and "panzerotti" (deep-fried calzones).

For a taste of Puglian pub culture, Bari Vecchia is a must-visit location because of its rustic ambiance and mouth watering food.

Craft Cocktails & Mixology

Puglia embraces its historic pub culture, but handmade cocktails and sophisticated mixology have also made their way into the region's establishments. In locations like Lecce and Ostuni, hip pubs and lounges offer imaginative cocktail menus that incorporate regional flavours and ingredients into inventive creations.

Enjoy a "Negroni" flavoured with bitter orange from Puglia or a "Martini Fiero" with a hint of rosé wine from Puglia as skilled bartenders demonstrate their abilities to create the ideal beverage.

Jazz Bars and Live Music

Puglia boasts a flourishing jazz and live music scene for visitors looking for a musical experience in addition to their drinks. Live performances are held at jazz clubs and music venues in towns like Brindisi and Taranto, creating the ideal atmosphere for an unforgettable night out.

Enjoy your favourite beverage in the company of other music lovers while listening to jazz, swing, and traditional Puglian music.

Coastal Beach Bars

Beach bars can be found all over Puglia's coastline, and they come alive in the summer. With umbrellas, sun loungers and a buzzing bar scene, these 'lidi' or beach clubs provide the classic beach experience.

Enjoy a refreshing "spuma" (Italian soda) or a "pugliese" cocktail (vodka, almond milk, and coffee) as you soak up the sun and the sea wind and get a taste of Puglia's relaxed coastal way of life.

The bar scene in Puglia is a celebration of life that provides a window into the region's rich cultural history, delectable culinary customs, and friendly hospitality. Every bar in Puglia has a different tale to tell, from the traditional 'passeggiata' to the fine art of aperitivo and the allure of caffè culture.

CHAPTER 6

Beaches

Puglia's environment is a captivating tapestry made of various elements and it is home to some of the most beautiful beaches in Italy. These breathtaking beaches in Puglia should be on your travel itinerary.

Baia delle Zagar

Baia delle Zagare is renowned for its white limestone cliffs, turquoise waters, and powdery sands. It is located inside the Gargano Peninsula. This quiet cove offers a paradisiacal hideaway where you may swim, sunbathe and take in the natural beauty. It is reachable via boat or a picturesque descent down the cliffs.

Torre dell'Orso

With its eye-catching twin sea stacks, known as "Le Due Sorelle," Torre dell'Orso offers a stunning coastal vista. The crystal-clear seas, soft dunes, and unusual rock formations combine to create a magical ambiance. While sunbathers can relax on the beach, adventurers can explore marine caverns.

Porto Cesareo Beach

This coastal jewel is known for its shallow, clear waters that resemble a sizable natural pool. You can marvel at a variety of aquatic life thanks to the protected marine region, which is a refuge for snorkelers and divers. Families will value the gently sloped shoreline, which provides a secure environment for kids to swim.

Punta Prosciutto

A quiet paradise of white dunes and green waters, Punta Prosciutto is tucked away on the Ionian coast. Its calm, shallow waters are ideal for swimming and wading. Sand dunes as a backdrop and a calm atmosphere offer a tranquil respite from the hustle and bustle of daily life.

Porto Selvaggio

Porto Selvaggio offers a magnificent coastal setting where the Mediterranean maquis grows. It is tucked away within a natural reserve. This unspoiled paradise is defined by rugged cliffs, secret coves, and crystal-clear waters. You may cool down in the inviting waters of the sea after taking a revitalising walk through the verdant surroundings.

Torre Lapillo

Frequently referred to as the "Maldives of Salento," Torre Lapillo is home to turquoise waters and ivory sands. It attracts beach enthusiasts because of its Caribbean-inspired aesthetics. The calm waves and modest slope make it ideal for swimming, tanning, and other water sports.

Baia dei Turchi

Baia dei Turchi, a spotless beach close to Otranto, is encircled by fragrant pine forests. Those looking for peace and a connection to nature are drawn to the unspoilt white sands and clear waters. It's the perfect place to unwind away from the crowds.

Porto Piatto

A hidden gem with a distinctive mix of sandy and rocky sections, Porto Piatto is a part of the Torre Guaceto Marine Reserve. For families to take a leisurely swim, it's a nice area to go because of the peaceful, shallow waters. For snorkelling fans, the rich undersea ecology is a heaven.

Pescoluse

Known as the "Maldives of Salento," Pescoluse is a popular beach resort thanks to its fine sands and vivid blue waters. There is plenty of room to play and unwind given the length of the shoreline. There are numerous beach clubs and other attractions in the neighbourhood, guaranteeing a relaxing and delightful visit.

Cala Porto Bianco

A hidden gem with crystal-clear waters and a wild vibe, Cala Porto Bianco is reachable by a picturesque walk through the Parco Naturale Regionale Terra delle Gravine. Its pebble beach is hidden within a quiet cove and provides a peaceful haven for nature enthusiasts.

Spiaggia di Porto Badisco

It's a stunning beach that is well-known for its crystal-clear blue waves and significant historical past. It is thought to be the location where the Trojan hero Aeneas set foot. The little bay has rugged cliffs surrounding it, creating a beautiful backdrop for swimming and snorkelling.

Torre Guaceto

Torre Guaceto is a natural coastal nature reserve with a complex ecology made up of sand dunes, wetlands, and crystal-clear waterways. For lovers of nature and birdwatching, it is a paradise. The beach is divided into several areas to accommodate both leisure time and water sports.

Cala dell'Acquaviva

This undiscovered gem is close to Marittima and can be reached along a charming trail that meanders among Mediterranean flora. The reward is a gorgeous pebble beach surrounded by rocks. The waters are ideal for swimming and snorkelling because they are so clear.

Cala Porto Rosso

This beach is renowned for its vivid red cliffs that strikingly contrast with the turquoise water. Your beach day will be made more exciting by the mountainous surroundings and the clean waters, which are perfect for swimming.

Spiaggia di Torre Pozzelle

This beach is encircled by historic watchtowers that stand as quiet sentinels. It is a well-liked location for families and snorkelers due to the shallow waters and rocky formations. The region has a lengthy history that dates back to the Roman era.

Porto Cavallo

This clean and remote beach is located within the Parco Naturale Regionale Terra delle Gravine. Pebbles and sand make up the beach, which is surrounded by verdant vegetation. It's a great location for nature enthusiasts seeking tranquilly due to the unspoiled surroundings.

Torre Colimena

This beach is close to a historic watchtower and is renowned for its mild, shallow waves. It's a wonderful location for families with young children because of its serene atmosphere. Long walks along the shoreline allow you to soak in the surrounding scenery.

Punta della Suina

This beach, which is close to Gallipoli, has both sandy stretches and rocky coves. Swimming in the shallow seas is perfect, and Mediterranean flora along the beach. Both locals and tourists love it because of the crystal-clear water and breathtaking views of the Gallipoli peninsula.

Baia di Porto Miggiano

This beach, which is close to Santa Cesarea Terme, is known for its rocky cliffs and crystal-clear seas. It's a great place for snorkelling and exploring because of the sea caves and rock structures. Additionally, you can unwind on the beach while admiring the breathtaking coastline vistas.

The sandy beach in Spaggia di Santa Maria al Bagno, which is close to Nard, offers a serene ambiance. Swimming in the crystal-clear seas is a breeze, and you can go to the town's historic district to browse local stores and eat delicious seafood.

Spiaggia di Punta Ristola

Puglia's southernmost beach can be found near Santa Maria di Leuca. The contrast between the rocky shoreline and the crystal-clear, turquoise waters is stunning. While taking in the sun and the water, you may also observe the historic "Fenicotteri" lighthouse.

Cala Verde

This is a remote beach encircled by limestone cliffs and Mediterranean vegetation, tucked away within the Parco Naturale Regionale Terra delle Gravine. It is the perfect getaway for nature enthusiasts due to its tranquil atmosphere and stunning surroundings.

Spiaggia di Portonuovo

This is a sandy beach that provides a tranquil retreat with breathtaking views of the Adriatic Sea. Swimming, lounging, and enjoying leisurely walks down the shore are all made possible by the golden sands and crystal-clear waters.

Each beach in Puglia has its own unique character and attraction. Puglia's beaches provide a wide variety of experiences that will leave you feeling amazed and rejuvenated, whether you're looking for adventure, leisure, or an opportunity to connect with nature.

CHAPTER 7

Outdoor Activities and Parks

Puglia is known for more than just its beautiful beaches and ancient cities. The area offers a wide variety of outdoor pursuits and recreational areas that entice adventurers, nature enthusiasts, and families to discover its natural wonders. The outdoor activities available in Puglia range from thrilling excursions to serene getaways. In this chapter, we cover all of the outdoor recreation opportunities and parks in Puglia to make sure your trip to this alluring locale is filled with unique adventures.

Puglia's Hiking and Trekking Trails

Outdoor enthusiasts and intrepid travellers are drawn to Puglia by its varied landscapes and fantastic hiking and trekking trails. The area provides a wide range of possibilities for anyone looking to fully immerse themselves in nature, from the untamed beauty of the Gargano National Park to the ancient landscapes of the Alta Murgia National Park. To make sure that your trip is full of wonderful experiences, we'll reveal the amazing hiking and trekking paths that are waiting for you in Puglia in this part of this book.

Gargano Coastal Trail

The breathtaking coastline of the Gargano Peninsula is lined with the Gargano Coastal Trail. On this trail, you can see imposing coastal cliffs, secret coves, and unspoiled beaches. Hikers can immerse themselves in the unmatched splendour of the Adriatic Sea by travelling from Vieste to Mattinata and finding hidden jewels along the way.

Sentiero Italia

Puglia is a part of the greater Sentiero Italia, the nation of Italy's longest hiking route. The Gargano National Park in Puglia is traversed by the trail, providing a singular opportunity to discover the area's varied landscapes, from ancient woods to coastal vistas.

Valle d'Itria Trails

There are beautiful routes in the Valle d'Itria that wind past vineyards, olive groves, and picturesque villages with trulli houses. To explore Puglia's rural core and to take in the pastoral scenery, walk from Alberobello to Locorotondo.

Foresta Umbra Trails

The Foresta Umbra is a lovely, old woodland with hiking routes. An idyllic atmosphere for wildlife exploration is provided by the cool shadow of ancient trees. To learn about the park's varied flora and fauna, stroll through the woods.

Monte Sant'Angelo Trails

To experience a spiritual ascension, walk to Monte Sant'Angelo, a popular pilgrimage destination. Along with breathtaking views of the Gargano coast, the route to the sanctuary provides a sense of connection to centuries of religious heritage.

Salerno Coastal Trails

The Ionian and Adriatic Seas' breathtaking splendour is displayed via Salento's seaside pathways. Explore the nearby shoreline to see spectacular coastal cliffs, undiscovered bays, and crystal-clear waters.

Caves of Castellana Trails

Explore the intricate system of underground caves known as the Caves of Castellana to go below earth. Guided excursions offer a distinctive trekking experience deep inside the earth as they lead you through breathtaking chambers decorated with stalactites and stalagmites.

Capo di Leuca Trails

The trails along Puglia's southernmost tip, Capo di Leuca, display a varied coastal topography. You can travel to the place where the Ionian and Adriatic Seas converge and explore it, taking in the breathtaking vistas as you go.

Selva di Fasano Trails

There are trails that weave through aromatic pine trees and lush oak forests in the Selva di Fasano, a green woodland region close to Alberobello. Hike across this magical setting to find ancient trulli hidden among the trees and secret streams.

Roca Vecchia Trails

Discover the coastal paths close to Roca Vecchia, where historical wonders and the sea meet. You'll come across historical ruins, churches carved out of rock, and caverns as you walk along the cliffs.

Torre Guaceto Marine Reserve Trails

Trails in the Torre Guaceto Marine Reserve take you through wetlands, coastal dunes, and Mediterranean vegetation. The reserve's numerous ecosystems shed light on the distinctive coastal ecology of Puglia.

Rauccio Park Trails

The Rauccio Park provides trails for city inhabitants seeking a green getaway. This urban paradise has covered places, gardens, and walking routes, making it the ideal place for a leisurely stroll.

Canale di Pirro Trails

Hike across the picturesque landscape along the Canale di Pirro, a historic aqueduct close to Bari. The route displays the rural beauty of the area while providing an insight into Puglia's history.

Alta Murgia Plateau Trails

The Alta Murgia Plateau's size makes for large trekking opportunities. You may genuinely connect with the rustic nature of the area on the trails, which provide broad vistas of rolling hills, farmland, and historical buildings.

Sant'Agata Park Trails

The Sant'Agata Park offers seaside pathways that meander among Mediterranean flora. These trails provide a peaceful respite with breath-taking sea vistas as your backdrop.

The hiking and trekking paths in Puglia provide a variety of views, from old woodlands to coastal panoramas. A different opportunity to connect with the area's natural beauty, history, and cultural legacy is presented by each route. You will discover the essence of Puglia's landscapes as you traverse these pathways and form lifelong memories of your outdoor experiences.

Cycling & Biking Adventures

Puglia is an ideal place for cyclists because of its level terrain. The region's riding prospects are as varied as they are alluring, ranging from coastal routes that provide glimpses of blue oceans to rural roads meandering past olive groves and attractive towns. This part of this book will show you the incredible bicycling destinations and cycling excursions Puglia has to offer, making sure your trip is full of thrilling adventures and stunning views.

Valle d'Itria

The Valle d'Itria provides bikers with a gorgeous backdrop with its recognisable trulli homes and rolling landscapes. Bike through the quaint towns of Alberobello, Locorotondo, and Cisternino, pausing to take in the historic buildings and breathtaking scenery.

Gargano National Park

On two wheels, tour the untamed splendour of the Gargano National Park. As you travel along the coast, you'll pass by secret coves, sea cliffs, and quaint fishing communities like Mattinata while enjoying magnificent views of the Adriatic Sea.

Acquedotto Puglise Route

Bicyclists go through Puglia's agricultural heartland on the Acquedotto Pugliese route. Take in the pastoral surroundings as you cycle through stunning olive orchards, vineyards, and farmland, all the while indulging in the area's world-famous cuisine.

Salento Peninsula

With its coastal routes that wind along the Ionian and Adriatic Seas, the Salento Peninsula beckons cyclists. Pedal from Oranto to Gallipoli while taking in the breathtaking scenery and cooling sea breeze.

The Adriatic Coastline

Numerous bicycle routes along the Adriatic coast offer unobstructed views of the water. From *Polignano a Mare* to *Monopoli*, ride along the coast, stopping at lovely beaches and sweeping vistas along the way.

Saline di Punta della Contessa

The Saline di Punta della Contessa, a nature preserve next to *Punta Prosciutto*, is accessible to cyclists and is famed for its salt pans and pink flamingos. Cycling is made easy by the reserve's level terrain and lovely surroundings.

Alta Murgia National Park

Bicyclists have the opportunity to bike through vast open expanses on the plains of the Alta Murgia National Park. Ride through trails that lead to historic rock churches and *masserie* to experience the distinctive karst nature of the area.

Taranto to Manduria

From Taranto to Manduria, cycle along the Ionian coast, passing through olive trees and charming coastal communities. This journey combines scenic views with learning about local cultures.

Riva dei Tessali to Marina di Ginosa

Riva dei Tessali to Marina di Ginosa, has a relaxing coastline ride. The route allows riders to enjoy the peace and quiet of the sea as it winds past pine trees and sandy beaches.

Altopiano della Murge

Cycling across the limestone plateau known as the Altopiano delle Murge is a fantastic experience. Explore the gently rolling terrain, travelling through historic towns and flowery meadows.

Brindisi to Ostuni

Brindisi, a maritime city, is reached by bicycle, as is the dazzling Ostuni, also known as the "White City." As you travel, cycle by vineyards and olive fields that highlight Puglia's agricultural heritage.

Trani to Barletta

Cycling along the coast from Trani to Barletta offers the chance to discover quaint beach communities and historic sites. As you travel along the coast, take in the breathtaking vistas of the Adriatic.

Taranto to Castellaneta

Travel through history on bicycle from Taranto to Castellaneta. You pass through scenic scenery, olive groves, and historic ruins on this trip.

Foggia to San Giovanni Rotondo

From Foggia, ride a bicycle to San Giovanni Rotondo, the city's spiritual hub. This route not only connects you to important religious places but also provides beautiful views of the surrounding landscape.

Lecce to Otranto

Set out on a bicycle trip from the baroque Lecce to the beach jewel of Oranto. This path mixes the stunning architecture of Lecce's ancient district with the stunning coastline and turquoise waters of Otranto.

Vieste to Peschici

From Vieste to Peschici, both located inside the Gargano National Park, you can bicycle along the seashore. The stunning views of the steep cliffs, sea caves, and the glistening Adriatic Sea are visible from the winding roadways.

Martina Franca to Cisternino

Discover the picturesque surroundings between the trulli-adorned towns of Cisternino and Martina Franca. Pedal through vineyards and olive groves while admiring the Valle d'Itria's picturesque countryside.

Litoranea Salentina

Several villages on the Salento Peninsula are connected by the picturesque seaside route known as the Litoranea Salentina. This route offers a variety of coastline views, charming villages, and historical sites for cyclists.

Bari to Monopoli

From the vibrant city of Bari, ride a bicycle to the quaint beach town of Monopoli. This route demonstrates Puglia's adaptability by providing a contrast between urban exploration and coastal relaxation.

Alberobello and Beyond

Start a loop in the area surrounding *Alberobello* that is covered in trulli. This cycling route gives you a sense of Puglia's natural splendour as you pass past olive groves, vineyards, and charming villages.

Polignano a Mare to Conversano

From the beautiful cliffs of Polignano a Mare, ride a bicycle to the ancient settlement of Converseno. This route skillfully combines the appeal of Conversano's mediaeval buildings with views of the coast.

Taranto to Lizzano

Bike from Taranto to Lizzano and take in the peace of Puglia's southern shore. The road passes by idyllic coastal villages, blue waters, and sandy beaches.

Brindisi to Mesagne

From Brindisi, ride a bicycle to Mesagne, a historic settlement. This route gives you an insight into Puglia's rich past as you pass through olive groves, vineyards, and age-old ruins.

Monopoli to Fasano

From the coastal town of Monopoli, bicycle to the picturesque countryside of Fasano. On this bicycle route, you may enjoy the lovely change from coastal views to rolling hills and classic Apulian buildings.

Saline di Margherita di Savoia

Discover Margherita di Savoia's salt pans and coastline splendour. Ride a bike across this extraordinary terrain, where the stark contrast between the blue sea and salt pans makes for a breathtaking sight.

Giovinazzo to Molfetta

Cycle from Giovinazzo to Molfetta along the Adriatic coast. This path passes through quaint beach communities, ancient harbours, and lovely scenery.

Monopoli to Castellana Grotte

By riding from Monopoli to Castellana Grotte, you may combine above-ground attractions with outdoor adventure. Before entering the interesting world of underground caves, cycle across the countryside.

Polignano a Mare to Alberobello

From the coastal splendour of Polignano a Mare, cycle to the trulli-dotted surroundings of Alberobello. This path provides the ideal blend of coastal views and rural charm.

Ceglie Messapica to Ostuni

Cycling from Ceglie Messapica to Ostuni is a hilly experience. While pedalling past vineyards and olive trees, take in the expansive views of the surroundings.

These varied riding and motorcycling routes in Puglia provide a multitude of activities, from country exploring to beach adventures. The riding paths in Puglia provide an enthralling ride into the centre of this magical region, whether you're looking for cultural immersion, scenic beauty, or a combination of both.

Horse Riding

When experienced on horseback, Puglia's rolling terrain, attractive countryside, and coastline beauties give a singular perspective. The natural splendour of Puglia may be experienced while horseback riding, including the region's olive trees, vineyards, picturesque villages, and sandy beaches. Here, we'll reveal the incredible locations in Puglia where you can go on horseback riding adventures, guaranteeing that your trip will be packed with magnificent scenery and unforgettable equestrian encounters.

Valle d'Itria

The Valle d'Itria is an alluring area to see on horseback because of its recognisable trulli buildings and rolling scenery. Discover the natural splendour of Locorotondo, Martina Franca, and Cisternino as you ride over the rolling hills, passing past olive trees and vineyards.

Gargano National Park

Get on your horse and ride around the breathtaking Gargano National Park. Canter through undiscovered beaches, sea cliffs, and quaint fishing communities like *Vi**este* as you traverse coastal pathways that provide panoramic views of the Adriatic Sea.

The Salento Peninsula

Equestrians are welcome to enjoy the Salento Peninsula's varied scenery. Experience the unique combination of coastal and rural beauty that characterises this region as you travel along sandy beaches, through olive groves, and through old towns.

Masserie Trails

By exploring the routes that wind past traditional masserie (farmhouses), you may ride through the heart of Puglia's agricultural legacy. You'll come to appreciate the rural appeal of the area as you stroll past vineyards and olive groves.

Fasano Countryside

On horseback, explore the Fasano countryside as you travel through vast olive trees and flower-filled meadows. You'll experience the adriatic breeze as you ride around and take in Puglia's pastoral splendour.

Castellana Grotte

Discover a distinctive horseback riding excursion close to Castellana Grotte. Before entering the underground world of the well-known Castellana caverns, you will take a horseback ride around the surrounding countryside.

Monopoli Coastal Ride

Riding along the sands in the vicinity of Monopoli, take in the splendour of the Adriatic coast. Canter along the sandy beaches while admiring the breathtaking coastal cliffs that serve as your ride's backdrop.

Altopiano delle Murge

The Altopiano delle Murge is a limestone plateau with amazing views, so saddle up for an adventure there. As you travel over the rolling terrain, you will encounter old farmhouses and ancient olive trees.

Sant'Agata Park

At the Sant'Agata Park, experience urban horseback riding. Trot through the greenery while still being surrounded by nature to experience the city from a different angle.

Coastal Dunes of Torre Canne

Take a peaceful ride among the beach dunes close to Torre Canne. Views of the turquoise water and the unspoiled natural beauty of the coastline will be your reward as you ride over the sandy trails.

Ceglie Messapica

Take to the saddle on "Ceglie Messapica" and see the surrounding area. Take a ride through countryside and olive trees before indulging in the regional cuisine that makes this quaint town so special.

Alta Murgia National Park

Horseback riders have the opportunity to explore the different landscapes of the Alta Murgia National

Park. Trot past historic locations as you pass through old forests, wide plains, and rugged terrain.

Marina di Lizzano

Enjoy the thrill of horseback riding along Marina di Lizzano's coastline. As you ride down the sandy shore and take in the breathtaking vistas of the Adriatic, enjoy the cooling sea breeze.

Polignano a Mare Clifftop Ride

The Adriatic Sea is visible from clifftops near Polignano a Mare as you ride along them. A distinctive vantage position to take in the seaside beauties is provided by this thrilling ride.

From beach gallops to rural treks, Puglia's amazing horseback riding locations provide a wide variety of experiences. Puglia's equestrian paths guarantee an authentic and unforgettable way to engage with the area's natural beauty, history, and local culture, regardless of whether you are an experienced rider or a beginner. You'll develop a strong bond with the landscapes as you ride through this alluring area, and you'll make priceless memories of your equestrian journeys.

Water Activities

Water sports aficionados will find Puglia to be the perfect vacation destination because to its breathtaking coastline, clear waters, and pleasant weather. The area offers a wide variety of water activities that let you fully immerse yourself in the Adriatic Sea, whether you're a beginner or an experienced pro. This part of this book reveals the incredible locations for water sports adventures that await you in Puglia, from exhilarating windsurfing sessions to tranquil kayaking explorations, guaranteeing that your aquatic voyage is full with excitement, relaxation, and unforgettable encounters.

Torre Guaceto Windsurfing

Windsurfing thrills can be had in Torre Guaceto Marine Protected Area. All levels of windsurfers can enjoy the optimum circumstances provided by the constant sea breeze and the still waters. Torre Guaceto is a windsurfing paradise for all skill levels thanks to its shallow waters and qualified instructors.

Kitesurfing at Porto Cesareo

Kitesurfing is a great activity at Porto Cesareo because of the crystal-clear waters. As you float over the waves while being driven by the wind and the force of your kite, feel the rush of adrenaline.

Both novice and seasoned kitesurfers can take advantage of the lessons offered by accredited institutions and enjoy this thrilling activity.

Santa Maria di Leuca Diving

Dive in Santa Maria di Leuca to discover Puglia's thriving underwater environment. Dive shops nearby offer expeditions to shipwrecks, reefs, and underwater caves. The marine richness and crystal-clear waters guarantee an unforgettable diving experience, regardless of your level of certification or prior diving experience.

Polignano a Mare Snorkelling

Snorkelling in the gorgeous waters of Polignano a Mare will allow you to discover the hidden gems below the surface. Explore underwater rock formations, swim with colourful fish, and take in the wonder of the Adriatic's marine life.

Kayaking in Baia delle Zagare

Launch a kayaking excursion in the Baia delle Zagare, close to Mattinata. Explore sea caves, isolated bays, and towering cliffs as you paddle around the rocky coastline. Kayaking is the perfect activity for spending time in nature because of the peace of the ocean and the spectacular vistas.

Sailing in Taranto

Sail the waterways of Taranto to embrace the nautical spirit. The tranquil water and gorgeous coastline offer an unforgettable sailing experience, regardless of whether you are an experienced or inexperienced sailor. Explore secret coves, old harbours, and quaint coastal towns by renting a boat.

Stand-Up Paddleboarding at Porto Selvaggio

Use a stand-up paddleboard (SUP) to travel the calm seas of Porto Selvaggio. Engage your core as you float over the tranquil water, admiring the breathtaking coastline scenery and the unspoiled beauty of the area.

Gallipoli Jet Skiing

Try jet skiing in the Gallipoli waters for a thrilling aquatic adventure. Feel the rush as you speed over the water, taking in the breathtaking scenery of the shoreline as you do so.

Water Skiing at Torre Canne

Water skiing is thrilling in Torre Canne. Skim across the water's surface while being towed by a boat, a demanding and thrilling water activity that combines skill and adrenaline.

Otranto Parasailing

You'll be propelled into the air by a parachute and experience the thrill of parasailing in Otranto. Make lifelong memories while taking in the town's breathtaking vistas and the glittering sea below.

Sea Kayaking in Polignano a Mare

Paddle among sea caverns and arches while sea kayaking in Polignano a Mare. Discover hidden gems that can only be reached by boat as you explore the beautiful shoreline from a fresh angle.

Monopoli Flyboarding
Flyboarding is a great way to express your inner superhero in Monopoli. Utilise water's ability to propel you above the waves so you can feel like you're flying while admiring the ocean's natural beauty.

Torre dell'Orso Water Biking

Water biking in Torre dell'Orso allows visitors to experience the blending of cycling and water activities. Pedal over the calm waves on specially made water bikes while taking in the seaside views.

Gallipoli Fishing Tours

Join a fishing tour in Gallipoli to experience traditional fishing. Cast your lines into the sea, pick up some local fishermen's tricks, and enjoy the delight of capturing your own seafood.

Paddle Yoga in Torre Guaceto

Try paddle yoga at Torre Guaceto to combine the peace of yoga with the calm of the sea. Practise yoga while floating on a paddleboard, connecting with the soft waves below you as you find balance and inner serenity.

Underwater Photography in Santa Cesarea Terme

In the clear waters of Santa Cesarea Terme, photography enthusiasts can learn the craft of underwater photography. Create enduring memories of your aquatic travels by capturing the colourful marine life and breathtaking seascapes.

Porto Badisco Fly Fishing

In Porto Badisco's crystal-clear waters, learn the skill of fly fishing. While surrounded by the natural beauty of the seaside area, cast your line and reel in a variety of fish species.

Brindisi Sailing Regattas

Participate in or watch sailing regattas hosted in the port city of Brindisi if you enjoy sailing. These thrilling tournaments show off expert sailors controlling their boats in exhilarating open-water races.

Otranto Hydrofoil Surfing

The thrill of surfing is increased to a whole new level by hydrofoiling, also known as foiling. On a hydrofoil board, glide above the water's surface as you ride the waves for more excitement and height.

Water Polo in Lecce

Play some exciting water polo in the city of Lecce. This competitive team sport mixes swimming, athleticism, and strategy, and it provides a fun way to spend time in the water with friends or fellow travellers.

Jet Blade in Gallipoli

Wearing special boots with water propulsion to elevate you above the sea's surface is required for the aquatic pastime known as jet blade. You will have an exciting and dynamic experience as you learn the skill of balance and control while being propelled by the force of the water.

Snuba Diving in Monopoli

In the crystal-clear seas of Monopoli, try snuba diving, a sport that combines scuba diving and snorkelling. Without the burden of bulky scuba gear, you can explore the underwater environment using a breathing apparatus attached to a floating raft.

Gallipoli Coastal Sailing

Discover secret coves, secluded beaches, and picturesque coastal towns as you sail along Gallipoli's coast. When you go coastal sailing, you may see Puglia's coastline from a different angle and get to places that are frequently inaccessible by land.

Porto Selvaggio Beach Volleyball

Play a game of beach volleyball at Porto Selvaggio to embrace the beach culture. The beautiful sea vistas and sandy sands make it the ideal setting for a friendly game in the sun.

Polignano a Mare Paddle Board Yoga
Paddle board yoga in the stunning Polignano a Mare waters is a test of balance and inner calm. Connect with the sea and the surrounding natural beauty by performing yoga poses while floating on a paddleboard.

Fishing with a Snorkel in Torre Guaceto

Go on a snorkel fishing experience at Torre Guaceto to combine snorkelling and fishing. Discover the undersea world, recognise various fish species, and attempt to capture some of your own food.

Kayak Polo in Gallipoli

Water polo and kayaking are combined to create the exciting and competitive team sport known as kayak polo. Attempt to score goals against the opposite team while paddling your kayak to create a thrilling aquatic duel.

Salento Canoe Tours

Take a canoe cruise along Salento's breathtaking coastline. Explore sea caves, paddle across calm seas, and find the undiscovered gems that define Puglia's coastal splendour.

Otranto's Subwing

Subwinging is an activity that involves being towed underwater while holding onto a subwing board. It has a distinct sensation. Enjoy an exciting and distinctive water journey while doing acrobatic manoeuvres and gliding across the water.

These outstanding water locations in Puglia provide a wide variety of aquatic experiences, from exhilarating thrills to peaceful explorations. Puglia's coastline ensures an unforgettable connection with the area's natural beauty and the Adriatic's dazzling waves, whether you're looking for exhilarating water sports or peaceful seaside moments. You'll make priceless memories and discover the allure of Puglia's aquatic environment as you dive, paddle, or sail across these alluring waterways.

Protected Nature Reserves

The natural splendour of Puglia is breathtaking, and the area is dedicated to protecting its distinctive ecosystems, wildlife, and landscapes. Puglia's protected natural areas provide as refuges for the region's indigenous plants and animals and give tourists an opportunity to experience the area's unspoiled beauty. Here, we'll examine the outstanding Puglian protected nature reserves that are waiting for you, guaranteeing that your trip is full of breathtaking interactions with nature, peace, and a profound appreciation for conservation efforts.

Torre Guaceto Marine Protected Area

A coastal treasure, the Torre Guaceto Marine Protected Area is home to pristine beaches, clean waters, and a wide variety of marine life. This reserve is a haven for underwater species, making it a well-liked location for diving, snorkelling, and taking in the natural beauty of the Mediterranean.

Alta Murgia National Park

The Alta Murgia National Park is a large area of unexplored wilderness that stretches across undulating hills and limestone plateaus. Unique rock formations, historic paths, and a wide variety of plant and animal species can all be found in the park's landscapes.

Salina di Margherita di Savoia

Birdwatchers and environment lovers will find this salt pan region to be a paradise. The Salina di Margherita di Savoia is a major wetland ecosystem that offers essential habitat for aquatic birds. It is home to a diversity of migratory and resident bird species.

Foresta Umbra in Gargano

The Foresta Umbra, a deep and old woodland within the Gargano National Park, is home to a diverse variety of plant and animal species. Visitors are enticed by the forest's lush beauty to explore its hiking routes and find secret springs and towering trees.

Porto Selvaggio Natural Park

The Porto Selvaggio Natural Park is tucked away along the coast and features turquoise waters and lush vegetation. This protected area offers isolated beaches for a tranquil coastal experience, hiking routes that lead to breath-taking seaside vistas, and breathtaking overlooks.

Palude del Conte and Duna Costiera

These networked nature reserves include coastal dunes, marshes, and salt pans. Palude del Conte and Duna Costiera are important bird habitats and present a rare chance to examine how land and water interact.

Bosco delle Pianelle

The protected woodland region known as Bosco delle Pianelle is distinguished by its lush foliage, winding trails, and serene ambiance. For those wanting a tranquil woodland experience, this natural refuge offers a tranquil respite.

Laghi Alimini

Two coastal lagoons make up Laghi Alimini, which provides a haven for both aquatic life and people looking to unwind. The lakes offer a magnificent backdrop for birdwatching, canoeing, and leisurely walks because they are surrounded by rich flora.

Area Marina Protetta Torre Sabea

As a haven for marine life and undersea ecosystems, this marine protected area includes both coastal and marine areas. Divers and snorkelers can explore the vibrant aquatic environment, while coastal trails offer beautiful treks.

Salento's Coastal Dunes

Due to their ecological importance and distinctive topography, Salento's coastal dunes are protected. Visitors can discover pristine coastal regions while these dunes provide habitat for plant species accustomed to sandy settings.

Riserva Naturale Statale delle Cesine

A large number of different bird species can be seen in the coastal marsh known as the Riserva Naturale Statale delle Cesine. The lagoons, reed beds, and sandy coasts of this reserve make it a popular spot for ecotourism and birdwatching.

Saltpans of Torre Colimena

Due to the region's significance for both biodiversity and cultural legacy, as well as the fact that these salt pans have been in use for millennia, it has been classified as a natural reserve. Visitors can take in the coastal views and see how traditional salt is produced.

Caves of Castellana

The Caves of Castellana offer a distinctive underground environment while not being a conventional nature reserve. Visitors can take guided excursions through these magnificent caves to see the unique rock formations and enigmatic chambers.

Oasis of Sant'Andrea Island

This tiny island in the Gulf of Taranto is an important resting place for migrating birds. The oasis is critical for bird conservation since it offers these birds a crucial resting spot when they are travelling.

Paludi di Ostuni

Numerous bird species and other fauna can be found in the combination of wetlands and salt pans known as the Paludi di Ostuni. The region was chosen as a protected nature reserve due to its biodiversity and cultural importance.

Pulo di Altamura

An unusual sinkhole surrounded by cliffs, caves, and rich vegetation is called Pulo di Altamura. Due to the significance of its archaeological value and the variety of flora and species that call it home, this natural wonder has been declared as a protected area.

Salina dei Monaci

A coastal lagoon called Salina dei Monaci is tucked away between the sea and sand dunes. The reserve is a good location for birding and monitoring the delicate balance of coastal ecosystems since its brackish waters provide habitat for a variety of bird species.

Cisternino Forest

A woodland notable for its ancient oak and beech trees is the Cisternino woodland. For those looking for tranquility in nature, this lush area provides quiet retreats, secret springs, and shaded trails.

Monte Conero Forest

The Monte Conero Forest, which is close to the town of Numana on the coast, provides an incredible fusion of woodland and sea vistas. The protected region has hiking routes that provide panoramic views of the Adriatic and is home to rare plant species.

Parco Naturale Regionale Bosco e Paludi di Rauccio

A variety of plant and animal species can be found in the marshes, woodlands, and water features that make up this regional park. Birdwatchers can see seasonal avian movements in Parco Naturale Regionale Bosco e Paludi di Rauccio, a crucial habitat for migratory birds.

Riserva Naturale Statale Torre Guaceto

This natural reserve protects the land area of Torre Guaceto, which is separate from the marine protected area. Visitors can get a sense of the region's terrestrial biodiversity by visiting the sand dunes, Mediterranean scrubland, and habitats that serve as homes for many animals and plants.

Bosco delle Pianelle

The peaceful surroundings of Bosco delle Pianelle are home to small animals, wildflowers, and oak trees. For those looking for seclusion, relaxation, and a closer connection to Puglia's natural surroundings, this tranquil forest is a refuge.

Parco Regionale Dune Costiere

A coastal region with sand dunes, Mediterranean plants, and beaches is called Parco Regionale Dune Costiere. This protected area serves as both a haven for plant and animal species that have evolved to this particular climate and a reminder of the value of protecting vulnerable coastal ecosystems.

Puglia's dedication to protecting its natural assets, diversified landscapes, and cultural riches is seen in these protected nature areas. Puglia's protected areas provide a variety of activities that link you with the beauty and relevance of the natural world, whether you're interested in seeing rare bird species, exploring ancient woodlands, or taking in geological wonders. You'll gain a deeper appreciation of the tenuous balance between human involvement and the environment as you travel through these areas.

Picnics and Relaxation

The parks and natural environs in Puglia provide peaceful locations for picnics and leisure. These tranquil retreats, which range from lush parks to beach getaways, provide a break from the busy world and let you savour the easy joys of leisure in Puglia's alluring surroundings.

Parco Naturale Regionale Bosco e Paludi di Rauccio

This regional park provides a variety of open spaces and shady locations, making it the perfect place for a picnic in the great outdoors. A calm setting for an outdoor lunch can be found at the Bosco e Paludi di Rauccio thanks to its serene ponds, winding trails, and lush forest.

Torre Guaceto Nature Reserve

The golden sands and grassy spaces next to the protected dunes make for the perfect locations for a picnic by the sea at Torre Guaceto. The sound of the waves will serenade you as you eat, and you'll be treated to the sight of azure waters spreading out in front of you.

Parco delle Dune Costiere.

This park's length along the Adriatic coast is punctuated by dunes, bushes, and walkways ideal for a tranquil picnic. You may take in both the refreshing sea breeze and the tranquil atmosphere of the inland environment at the Parco delle Dune Costiere.

Lecce's Historic Gardens

There are numerous antique gardens in Lecce that offer a tranquil setting for relaxation. For instance, the Giardini Pubblici di Lecce has lovely statues, decorative flora, and exquisite gazebos that beckon you to relax for a while.

Parco di Villa Castelli

This park is found in the Villa Castelli town and features a lovely lake and inviting picnic areas. Your outdoor lunch is set against a tranquil backdrop of beautiful surroundings and the sound of water, providing an opportunity to relax and get away.

Grottaglie's Historical Centre

Grottaglie's charming streets and piazzas make the ideal location for an outdoor picnic. The blend of regional flavours and the allure of this quaint town can be enjoyed by setting up your spread in a cosy corner of the historical centre.

Parco Belvedere Marconi, Monopoli

Parco Belvedere Marconi, which offers a tranquil hideaway for picnicking and overlooks the Adriatic Sea. An attractive atmosphere to have a leisurely dinner while staring out at the boundless blue horizon is created by the park's well-kept lawns and panoramic vistas.

Masseria Brancati

Picnics can be enjoyed in tranquil settings at some of Puglia's antique masserie (farmhouses). You can take pleasure in a leisurely meal amidst the natural beauty of the area at Masseria Brancati, for instance, which features wide lawns, ancient olive trees, and rustic charm.

Trani's Seaside Promenade.

A well-liked location for relaxing and picnicking is Trani's Lungomare Cristoforo Colombo, a picturesque promenade along the sea. Spread yourself on the grassy or bench-covered areas as you take in the magnificent Trani Cathedral and the serene Adriatic Sea.

Parco di Villa Comunale

Foggia's Parco di Villa Comunale city park provides a peaceful haven in the middle of the city. A peaceful picnic in the middle of the city is made possible by the park's fountains, green lawns, and tree-lined walks.

Punta della Suina Beach

Punta della Suina near Gallipoli offers a tranquil beach location for a more private lunch by the sea. This location allows you to enjoy your picnic in seclusion and take in the beauty of the coastal area as it is tucked between rugged cliffs and sparkling waves.

Ostuni's Terraces

There are quiet spots for a picnic amid Ostuni's winding streets and terraces. In the midst of Ostuni's famous white architecture, locate a position with a view of the charming village perched against the hillside.

Specchia's Historic Square

The piazza in the centre of Specchia is a lovely location for a picnic. This area offers the ideal setting for a laid-back outdoor supper, surrounded by ancient buildings, quaint eateries, and a sense of a close-knit community.

Selva di Fasano

A picnic in the tranquility of nature is possible in the wooded area of Selva di Fasano. You can have a quiet supper and take in the calming sounds of the forest if you choose a quiet area under the trees.

Parco Belloluogo

Parco Belloluogo offers a city park where you may take a leisurely picnic between trees and gardens. The calm of the park provides a nice respite from the bustle of the city.

Porto Selvaggio Natural Park

Natural park Porto Selvaggio, located close to Nard, offers a rocky coastal environment and secret coves where you may enjoy a private picnic by the sea. Enjoy your dinner while being surrounded by Puglia's untamed natural beauty.

Parco Canale di Pirro in San Giovanni Rotondo

San Giovanni Rotondo's canal-side park provides a tranquil setting for a picnic that is bordered by water and vegetation. The park's benches, walkways, and serene ambiance make it a relaxing place to spend some time.

Valle d'Itria countryside

Find a peaceful area in the Valle d'Itria's lovely landscape, perhaps next to a typical trullo. These rural areas, whether in Cisternino, Locorotondo, or Alberobello, provide a chance to commune with nature and have a tranquil picnic.

You're invited to unwind, enjoy regional cuisine, and take in the peace and quiet at these serene picnic and relaxing locations in Puglia. Each of these retreats offers a special opportunity to embrace the art of relaxation and find comfort in the beauty of Puglia's landscapes, whether you prefer to enjoy a coastal breeze, a historical setting, or a quiet park.

Camping and Glamping

Camping and glamping provide the ideal balance of outdoor adventure and comfort for people looking for a closer relationship with nature and a distinctive way to see Puglia's landscapes. Puglia offers a variety of options for experiencing the region's natural beauty while enjoying the comforts that fit your preferences, ranging from conventional campgrounds to opulent glamping locations.

Camping La Masseria

Camping La Masseria, located close to Gallipoli, provides a beachfront camping experience with easy access to a sandy beach. Camping enthusiasts can pitch their tents or park their campers among olive trees and take in the serene surroundings and mesmerising views of the Adriatic Sea.

Torre Rinalda Camping Village

Campers can find a beach sanctuary at Torre Rinalda Camping Village, which provides views of the Ionian Sea. Use the facilities at the campground, which include restaurants, bars, and swimming pools, and decide between classic tent camping and a cosy mobile home.

Agricamping Tenuta Tredici Ulivi

Agricamping Tenuta Tredici Ulivi offers a basic camping experience amidst an olive grove.. At this environmentally friendly campground, you can stay in an elegant trulli or bring your own tent and get close to nature.

Glamping Puglia Village

Glamping Puglia Village in Monopoli provides a selection of opulent lodgings for people looking for a little luxury in the great outdoors. These fashionable options, which range from yurts to safari tents, offer hotel-like conveniences while immersing you in the grandeur of nature.

Camping Lamaforca

Camping Lamaforca, a family-friendly campground, provides a variety of camping alternatives, such as mobile homes and campsites for tents or campers. Take advantage of the fun things to do, entertainment, and easy access to the Adriatic's pristine seas.

Agricamping Terra Etrusca

Agricamping Terra Etrusca is a peaceful getaway in the countryside close to Manduria. Large plots, farm-fresh food, and a calm environment provide for a camping experience that is genuinely enjoyable.

Glamping Torre Sant'Andrea

Glamping Torre Sant'Andrea in Otranto offers opulent tents and a prime site by the sea for glamping fans seeking a coastal experience. Immerse yourself in opulent comfort while also enjoying the beauty of nature.

Camping Village Baia degli Aranci

The Vieste campground, Camping Village Baia degli Aranci, provides an exciting camping environment beside the Adriatic Sea. This campground offers an all-inclusive getaway for both families and adventure seekers with a variety of amenities like swimming pools, restaurants, and sports fields.

These camping and glamping options broaden the selection of lodgings offered in Puglia and let visitors tailor their outdoor experience to suit their interests. Puglia's camping and glamping locations provide an authentic and immersive approach to take in the area's natural beauty.

Stargazing in Puglia

Puglia's expansive landscapes, low levels of light pollution, and bright skies make it the perfect location for astronomy aficionados to view the night sky's wonders. The area has several places where visitors can view the celestial splendour above, from the rustic appeal of rural countryside to the serene seaside stretches.

Gargano National Park

The Gargano Peninsula is a top spot for astronomy because of its isolation and protected status. To see the bright stars that light up the night sky, find a calm area in the national park that is far from any lights from the city.

Salento's Coastal Retreats

The coastal regions of Salento provide a singular opportunity to experience both astronomy and the calming sounds of the water. Select a beach or a seaside promenade to take in the captivating sight of the stars reflected in the water.

Valle d'Itria's Countryside

Get away to the Valle d'Itria's rural areas where the absence of city lights makes it possible for the stars to shine brightly. Enjoy the serenity of the countryside vistas while observing the planets and constellations.

Grotte di Castellana

When night falls, step outside to see the stars above the old rock formations. During the day, explore the wonderful underground world of the Grotte di Castellana. It's impossible to forget this experience because of the way that caves and celestial splendour combine.

Otranto's Historic Centre

In the evening, stroll through the quaint alleyways of Otranto's old district before finding a seat in a piazza to see the night sky. Your experience of stargazing will be enhanced by the contrast between the cosmic wonders above and the old architecture.

Bosco Selva

Go to Bosco Selva for a close encounter with the natural world and the stars. This wooded region, close to Mesagne, offers a tranquil setting for stargazing amidst the trees and the sounds of the forest.

Torre Guaceto Nature Reserve

Stargazing is made possible by the clean surroundings and coastal setting of the Torre Guaceto Nature Reserve. Visitors can take in the grandeur of the night sky away from city lights on the beach or within the reserve's grounds.

Parco Nazionale Alta Murgia

Parco Nazionale Alta Murgia, designated as an International Dark Sky Park, provides superb viewing conditions. Visitors can get clear views of the cosmos from authorised observation spots.

Porto Selvaggio Natural Park

Porto Selvaggio Natural Park, located along the Ionian Coast, combines the attractiveness of the coast with celestial splendour. To see the stars reflecting on the water, pick a location near some cliffs or the ocean.

Castel del Monte

From Castel del Monte, a UNESCO World Heritage site, see the night sky. You may enjoy astronomy from a special vantage point while being surrounded by history at this famous fortification.

Specchia

An intimate location for stargazing can be found in the small village of Specchia in the Salento area. You are able to truly appreciate the heavenly splendour above because there are no city lights around.

Punta Prosciutto Beach

This beautiful beach in Porto Cesareo provides a calm atmosphere for stargazing. Spread out a blanket on the gentle sands and take in the serene ambiance while gazing up at the stars.

Alberobello's Trulli

From this old village, take in the trulli's distinctive architecture as you stare up at the stars. The interesting contrast between the conical roofs and the cosmic void is created.

Parco Naturale Regionale Terra delle Gravine

Find a quiet space in this regional park that encompasses Taranto and Brindisi. The park's varied landscapes offer the perfect setting for establishing a cosmic connection.

Marina di Pulsano

The Ionian Coast town of Marina di Pulsano provides a serene seaside setting for stargazing. Your cosmic voyage is accompanied by the relaxing sound of the waves.

The calm surroundings and beautiful skies of Puglia provide the ideal backdrop for stargazers to enjoy the wonders of the night sky. These places offer a cosmic journey that is sure to leave you in awe of the wonders of the universe, whether you are drawn to coastal vistas, ancient architecture, or the centre of rural tranquility.

Birdwatching

For those who enjoy birdwatching, Puglia's varied landscapes—which include coastal sections, wetlands, woodlands, and rural areas—offer a haven. Due to its advantageous location along bird migration routes, the area receives a variety of avian species all year long. Puglia's natural ecosystems offer an unparalleled opportunity to see and enjoy the beauty of its avian residents, from mighty migratory birds to majestic birds of prey.

Salina dei Monaci

Salina dei Monaci is a coastal lagoon that draws a wide range of bird species. It is situated in the centre of the regional park of Porto Cesareo. Flamingos, herons, waders, and other waterbirds can find perfect feeding grounds in the salt pans and marshes.

Lago di Lesina and Lago di Varano

For birdwatchers, these two coastal lagoons are a haven. An excellent location for seeing both resident and migratory birds, the wetlands and mudflats draw spoonbills, marsh harriers, and glossy ibises.

Alta Murgia National Park

Birds of prey find the broad vistas and rocky outcrops of this park to be the ideal habitat. Watch for kestrels, peregrine falcons, and Bonelli's eagles flying overhead.

Lago Salso

Lago Salso, a crucial wetland habitat for many bird species, is located halfway between Taranto and Brindisi. When birds are migrating, the area turns into a hotspot for birdwatching since so many waders and waterfowl pass through.

Bosco Incoronata

Songbird lovers will love this forest close to Cerignola. Bosco Incoronata is alive with the sounds of these lovely birds, from nightingales to golden orioles.

Torre Guaceto Nature Reserve

Along with its stunning coastline, Torre Guaceto is a sanctuary for birdwatchers. During their annual migrations, migratory birds like terns, sandpipers, and plovers are drawn to the wetlands and sand dunes.

Gargano National Park

The abundant birdlife of Gargano National Park is a part of its great biodiversity. Rock thrushes, red-billed choughs, and black kites all have habitats in the coastal cliffs and forests.

Margherita di Savoia Salt Pans

Not only are these salt pans an industrial area, but they are also a haven for several bird species. A variety of waders, including sandpipers and stints, are drawn to the mudflats and shallow seas.

Valle d'Itria

Valle d'Itria's rural settings provide a serene environment for birdwatching. Discover kestrels, hoopoes, and European rollers by exploring the fields, vineyards, and olive groves.

Parco Naturale Regionale delle Dune Costiere da Torre Canne a Torre San Leonardo

This regional park, which stretches along the coast, has a variety of ecosystems that are home to several bird species. You'll find a range of feathered occupants, from larks to wheatears.

The distinctive combination of coastal regions, marshes, forests, and rural landscapes in Puglia offers birding aficionados a wide range of chances. These places provide a window into the avian richness that coexists with the area's natural beauty, whether you're a serious birder or just a casual observer.

There are several possibilities to interact with the landscapes, fauna, and cultural history of Puglia through outdoor pursuits. Whatever your travel preferences, Puglia has a lot to offer.

CHAPTER 8

Cultural Attractions

Puglia is a land of several cultural attractions which are capable of making your journey worthwhile.

Puglian Festivals

The exuberant celebrations of Puglia's festivals reflect the region's strong character, long-standing traditions, and rich cultural history. The area comes alive all year long with a wide variety of festivals that highlight its history, music, dancing, cuisine, and religious devotion. Puglia's festivals provide tourists with an entire experience that promotes a stronger connection to the region's identity, from the gorgeous alleys of old towns to the bustling coastlines of its coastal communities.

Le Festa di San Nicola (Bari)

San Nicola, the patron saint of Bari, is honoured with fervour and elaborate processions. Religious rituals, parades, and the transfer of his remains from the Basilica of San Nicola to the waterfront are all part of the festivities.

La Festa della Taranta (Salento) August

The Festa della Taranta is a vibrant music event that honours the Pizzica dance, which is unique to Puglia. Around the world, musicians congregate in various cities, leading up to a huge concert in Melpignano.

La Notte della Taranta (Salento) August

This folk music festival honours the Pizzica dance and presents Salento's traditional dance and music. For a night of music, dancing, and cultural immersion, hundreds of guests go to Melpignano for the finale.

Sagra delle Orecchiette (Ceglie Messapica) August

Sagra delle Orecchiette by Ceglie Messapica honours Puglian cuisine, particularly the renowned pasta form. The festival offers food stalls, cultural acts, and cookery demos.

Processione dei Misteri, Good Friday

The Processione dei Misteri, a lavish Good Friday parade with magnificent floats portraying events from the Passion of Christ, is a stirring demonstration of faith and artistic talent.

La Sagra della Purità, August

This event honours the Virgin Mary with processions, concerts, and cultural dances that enthral both residents and tourists.

Infiorata di Conversano (Conversano) Corpus Christi

For the Corpus Christi celebrations, the Infiorata di Conversano, a magnificent floral carpet with elaborate designs, fills the town's streets.

Sagra del Fico Mandorlato, August

The Sagra del Fico Mandorlato features food tastings, exhibits, and cultural performances to honour the area's sweets made with figs and almonds.

La Festa di Sant'Oronzo (Lecce) August 24

The Festa di Sant'Oronzo in Lecce celebrates the patron saint of the city with religious processions, cultural activities, and an impressive fireworks show.

Fiera del Levante (Bari) September

The Fiera del Levante in Bari is a sizable trade expo that highlights the economic and agricultural accomplishments of the area. It's a chance to see Puglia's thriving economy.

Festa di San Martino (Oria) November 11

The Festa di San Martino in Oria honours the town's patron saint by bringing the neighbourhood together through a variety of religious processions, musical performances, and cultural activities.

Festa di San Cataldo (Taranto) May 10

The Festa di San Cataldo in Taranto celebrates the patron saint with religious rites, processions, and a joyous environment that unites locals and tourists.

Carnevale di Fasano (Fasano) February.

Fasano's Carnevale is a vibrant celebration that encapsulates the joyous spirit of the season with parades, masked balls, and energetic street acts.

The festivals of Puglia offer a singular window into the region's cultural identity, giving visitors a chance to engage with local customs, take in exuberant celebrations, and take part in the happiness of social gatherings.

Galleries and Museums in Puglia

The numerous galleries and museums in Puglia beautifully preserve the region's rich historical past and dynamic cultural landscape. These places provide visitors with an immersive experience that highlights the region's unique heritage and artistic expression, showcasing anything from archaeological treasures to modern art. Puglia's galleries and museums offer a riveting look into the heart and spirit of the region, whether you're interested in ancient history, exquisite art, or regional traditions.

Museo Archeologico Nazionale (Taranto)

This museum is home to a remarkable collection of artefacts that chronicle Magna Graecia's history. The museum provides insights into the ancient civilizations that previously predominated in the area, from Greek pottery and sculpture to Roman mosaics.

Castello Svevo (Bari), Italy

The Gipsoteca, a display of casts of local sculptures, is located in the mediaeval fortification known as the Swabian Castle in Bari. The castle itself is a work of art in terms of architecture, providing sweeping vistas over the city.

Museo Civico (Ostuni)

The Civic Museum in Ostuni exhibits the town's historical and artistic heritage using artefacts from the past, including mediaeval manuscripts and archaeological finds. The arrangement of the museum provides a historical tour of Ostuni's past.

Museo Faggiano (Lecce)

The Museo Faggiano in Lecce is a treasure trove of archaeological artefacts that chronicles a find made while remodelling a structure. History can be explored in layers, from mediaeval artefacts to Roman remnants.

Museo Archeologico Nazionale di Ugento (Ugento)

The National Archaeological Museum in Ugento exhibits artefacts from the Mesopotamian, Roman, and prehistoric eras. The museum's numerous displays provide a thorough look into the area's prehistoric past.

Museo della Ceramica (Grottaglie)

The pottery-making heritage of the town is honoured in Grottaglie's Ceramic Museum. Visitors can take in the beautiful ceramics on display and discover the generations-old artistry.

Museo Civico (Altamura)

The archaeological discoveries made in the town, including artefacts from prehistoric eras, are shown in Altamura's Civic Museum. The investigation into the area's prehistoric past is fascinating.

Museo del Mare "Spazio Porto" (Gallipoli)

This Sea Museum in Gallipoli provides information about the town's marine past, fishing customs, and seafaring culture. The displays highlight the town's close ties to the ocean.

Museo Etnografico della Civiltà Contadina (Ruffano)

The customs, equipment, and way of life of Puglia's rural communities are highlighted in Ruffano's Ethnographic Museum of Peasant Culture. It pays homage to the area's agricultural past.

Museo Diocesano (Andria)

The religious artefacts, paintings, and sculptures in Andria's Diocesan Museum are a reflection of the town's spiritual heritage and artistic accomplishments.

Puglia's galleries and museums offer a fascinating trip through time and culture, showcasing everything from ancient artefacts to modern innovations. They offer a forum for people and tourists to interact with the history, present, and future of the area, creating a greater understanding of Puglia's creative and historical legacy.

CHAPTER 9

Children's Activities and Attractions in Puglia

Puglia has a wide range of activities and attractions for families travelling with kids, thanks to its beautiful landscapes, lively culture, and friendly residents. Young visitors will have a fun and educational trip to Puglia thanks to the region's kid-friendly activities, which range from exploring historic castles to taking part in outdoor excursions. Every child explorer can find something to pique their interest in Puglia, whether it be exploring quaint towns, unwinding on sand beaches, or participating in interactive learning.

Castles and Fairy Tales

Young explorers' imaginations are sparked by the magnificent castles in Puglia. The renowned 13th-century castle known as Castel del Monte, which is a UNESCO World Heritage site, is distinguished by its unusual octagonal shape. There are opportunities to travel back in time and envision mediaeval experiences at the Castello Aragonese in Taranto and the Oria Castle.

Playful Sands and Beach Days

Family-friendly beaches can be found all over Puglia's coastline where children may construct sandcastles, paddle in the calm waves, and enjoy the sunshine. Popular beaches with clean, safe areas for kids to play and experience the joys of the sea include Torre Guaceto, Baia dei Turchi, and Punta Prosciutto.

ZooSafari Fasanolandia

Children can see exotic creatures up close at ZooSafari Fasanolandia, a distinctive animal park. They are introduced to lions, giraffes, and other animals at the drive-through safari, and there are rides, shows, and play spaces for kids of all ages in the amusement park area.

Grotte di Castellana

At the Grotte di Castellana, a fascinating cave network with amazing structures, go on an underground adventure. Families can experience awe-inspiring chambers on guided tours, where kids can be inspired by the wonders of nature.

Acquapark Egnazia's Water Park Entertainment

Water-based fun is available at Acquapark Egnazia, which features pools, slides, and other attractions for kids of all ages. It's the ideal location for a day of fun for the whole family while staying cool.

Trulli Explorations in Alberobello and Beyond

It might be like walking into a village from a fantasy when you visit Alberobello because of its distinctive trulli buildings. Children may learn about the history of these unusual cone-shaped homes while exploring them. The nearby Trulli of Castellana offers yet another chance to explore conventional Puglian architecture.

Egnazia Archaeological Park

Families can discover historical ruins at Egnazia Archaeological Park, including a Roman city and a Messapian hamlet, while having fun and learning new things. History is brought to life for young minds through interactive exhibitions and guided tours.

Torre Guaceto and Bosco Selva Nature Reserves

Children have the opportunity to connect with nature at places like Torre Guaceto and Bosco Selva. Children can learn about the region's flora and animals in an interesting way through guided tours, wildlife spotting, and educational programmes.

Amusing Workshops for Crafts and Cooking

Kids have the opportunity to take cooking classes and prepare regional specialties like orecchiette pasta thanks to Puglia's culinary traditions. They are also introduced to regional arts and crafts, such as ceramics and painting, through craft programmes.

Festivities and Events

Festivals in Puglia frequently feature activities for the whole family, like processions, parades, and musical performances. For kids, participating in the local culture during these celebrations helps to establish enduring memories.

Il Parco Avventura Lama d'Antico

An adventure park featuring climbing obstacles, ropes courses, and zip lines is called Il Parco Avventura Lama d'Antico. It's a wonderful method for families to engage in outdoor activities.

Educational Farms

Children can engage with animals, learn about farming, and experience rural life directly at educational farms, or "masserie didattiche." These farms include outdoor activities, workshops, and guided tours.

Safe Cycling for Families

Puglia is perfect for family bike excursions because of its level terrain and picturesque pathways. Take your time cycling along the coast, across the countryside, and through the quaint villages.

Dinosaur Park

The prehistoric world comes to life for young explorers at this dinosaur-themed park, which features life-sized models of dinosaurs, interactive exhibits, and educational activities.

Castello Normanno-Svevo (Bari)

Bari's Norman-Swabian Castle offers interactive displays, activities, and mediaeval architecture that let children experience life as a knight, king, or queen.

Parco del Negroamaro

Parco del Negroamaro is an amusement park with a wine theme that involves children in a fun and instructive activity while educating them about Puglian wine culture through hands-on exhibits.

Adventure Park, Gomma Piuma (Bari)

This Bari adventure park has trampolines, obstacle courses, and inflatable playgrounds that keep kids of all ages entertained for hours.

Every member of the family, from the smallest to the oldest, may have a fulfilling and enriching vacation, thanks to Puglia's family-friendly activities and attractions. Puglia offers a variety of activities that encourage great family time and help build priceless memories, whether you're touring historic places, going on outdoor excursions, or participating in interactive learning.

CHAPTER 10

Other Important Information

Language

Travellers are able to access Puglia's heart and soul through the language. Puglia's cultural diversity and historical influences have affected the use of dialects and local languages, albeit Italian is the region's official language. The ability to negotiate Puglia's language terrain improves the traveler's ability to interact with locals, comprehend cultural nuances, and forge deep connections.

Italian is widely spoken and understood across Puglia and is the national language of Italy. For tourists, being able to communicate and get around in daily life is substantially improved by possessing a basic command of Italian phrases. A few basic Italian phrases can go a long way in promoting friendly encounters and demonstrating cultural respect, whether ordering food at a neighbourhood trattoria or asking for directions in the picturesque alleyways of Alberobello.

Also, the employment of several dialects in Puglia, in addition to Italian, reflects the region's rich cultural legacy. Apulian dialects give the area's linguistic landscape depth and richness because they are shaped by historical events and interactions with neighbouring regions. Even among the same cities and villages, dialects can vary, highlighting the distinct cultural identity of each community. Interacting with people in their dialects can result in sincere and meaningful conversations that provide light on the history and customs of the area.

Beyond Italian and dialects, Puglian slang also includes particular words and expressions with a strong cultural foundation. These phrases capture the essence of Puglia's way of life, from agricultural terminology like "masseria" (ancient farmstead) to culinary terms like "orecchiette" (little ear-shaped pasta). Understanding and employing these regional terminology not only makes it easier for visitors to get around, but it also shows a sincere interest in the culture and history of the area.

Travellers' Advice on Communicating and Connecting

- Learn some basic Italian greetings, directions, food ordering, and expressions of gratitude before your trip. Locals will value your efforts, and your conversations will go more smoothly.

- Even while it's not required, picking up a few words in the local accent can be a pleasant and rewarding way to interact with locals. It demonstrates a sincere interest in their way of life.

- Use Nonverbal Communication. Nonverbal cues like gestures and expressions on the face are understood by all people. Puglia is noted for its expressive body language, making it easier to communicate by observing and copying native gestures.

- Start up talks with restaurant employees, shops, and other patrons. Engaging with Pugliese people might result in remarkable interactions because they are renowned for their warmth and friendliness.

- Even if you don't speak Italian well, making an effort to communicate and respecting the local tongue will go a long way. Locals frequently recognise the effort and are eager to help.

- While travelling, phrasebooks and language learning applications can be really helpful. They can aid in navigating real-world circumstances and provide meaning for cultural quirks.

- Understanding regional conventions and norms might improve your communication because language and culture are interwoven. For instance, Pugliese people share the reputation of Italians for having expressive communication styles.

Language in Puglia is a key that opens doors to real experiences, cultural knowledge, and enduring memories rather than just a tool for communication. The linguistic diversity of Puglia improves your tour and enables you to genuinely connect with the essence of the area, whether you're speaking Italian, utilising dialects, or using local phrases.

Safety and Emergency Contacts

Puglia travel promises stunning scenery, a fascinating past, and a lively culture. While you're probably concentrating on exploring and having fun, safety must come first. A secure and worry-free voyage through this captivating region is ensured by familiarising yourself with safety precautions, regional customs, and emergency contacts.

General Safety Advice

- Learn as much as you can about the places you intend to visit, including their customs, laws, and potential security risks. You can avoid dangerous circumstances and make educated decisions if you are well-informed.

- Like any other place you might visit, it is wise to protect your possessions. For your valuables, use hotel safes or locks that are secure, and stay away from flashing expensive jewellery or devices.

- The hot, sunny weather in Puglia can be oppressive, especially in the summer. To protect yourself from the sun, drink enough water, put on sunscreen, and dress in proper attire.

- Comply with all local rules and ordinances. When visiting churches, temples, or other places of worship in Puglia, keep in mind the local traditions and clothing regulations.

- For dependable and safe transportation, use licenced taxis, ride-sharing services, or reputed automobile rental providers. Make sure the regions where you stay are viewed properly.

- Use a mobile phone that is well charged and has a local SIM card or international roaming to stay in touch. Make sure to preserve critical contacts and offline maps.

Who to Contact in Case of Emergency

It's essential to keep the appropriate contacts close to hand in case of an emergency. Here are some crucial figures to have in mind while in Puglia:

- To contact emergency services, including police, fire, and ambulance, dial 112. You can reach the proper service in Italy by calling this general emergency number.

- For non-urgent concerns, go to the closest Carabinieri station or call 112 for general emergencies. They support the community and uphold public safety.

- Medical Support: Call 118 to request an ambulance in case of medical emergencies. In order to offer care, hospitals and other medical institutions are well-equipped.

- There are specific police stations for tourists in some tourist locations. They can offer support and information geared towards travellers.

Also, know the address and phone number of your country's embassy or consulate in advance if you are a foreign national and need assistance.

Safety Precautions

- Important Documents Should Be Copied Make copies of your passport, ID, and travel insurance and keep them safe. Keep them away from the originals when storing.

- Be Conscious of Your Environment: Keep an eye out for danger whether you're in the tranquil countryside or the bustling city.

- While Puglia's public transit is mostly secure, be on the lookout for pickpockets when travelling in crowded environments like buses and trains.

- Find out which medical facilities, pharmacies, and hospitals are closest to your lodging.

- Have a collection of fundamental emergency words and phrases in Italian on hand to use in urgent situations.

- Share your itinerary, lodging preferences, and contact information with a close relative or friend. Regular check-ins add an additional level of security.

Although Puglia is a safe place to visit, accidents can happen anywhere. A smooth and safe trip can be made by being well-informed, taking safety precautions, and being aware of who to call in an emergency. By putting safety first, you may fully enjoy all that Puglia has to offer in terms of beauty and wonder while preserving your health as a top priority.

Health and Wellness

In addition to breathtaking scenery and a thriving cultural scene, a trip to Puglia offers the chance to put your health and wellbeing first. Maintaining your physical and emotional wellness is crucial as you take in the splendour of the area. Puglia offers a complete tourist experience that nourishes the body and the soul, from comprehending local healthcare to remaining active and embracing wellness practises.

Medical Services Navigation

The well-established healthcare system in Puglia makes sure that visitors may get high-quality treatment when they need it. Consider the following important elements when looking into Puglian healthcare:

- Hospitals, clinics, and medical facilities in Puglia offer a variety of healthcare services. Larger cities with established medical facilities include Bari, Lecce, and Brindisi.

- Pharmacies (farmacie) are prevalent in the towns and cities of Puglia. They sell both prescription and over-the-counter medicines. Keep an eye out for the green cross.

- Health Insurance It is advisable for travellers to have complete travel insurance that includes medical emergencies. Verify your policy's coverage for hospitalisation, medical evacuation, and medical costs.

- Despite the fact that English is spoken in tourist destinations, it can be useful to have a translation tool or a dictionary on hand to clearly express medical concerns.

- If you need to take any particular drugs, pack enough to last the duration of your vacation. To prevent any problems at customs, bring medications and a doctor's note.

Practises for Wellness

- Mediterranean food from Puglia is not only delicious but also nutritious. Enjoy fresh veggies, olive oil, seafood, and local foods to maintain a healthy diet.

- Puglia has beautiful scenery that is conducive to outdoor pursuits like swimming, cycling, and walking. Staying active is simple, whether it's taking a leisurely stroll through a historical town or an energising walk along the seaside.

- The tranquil landscape and lovely beaches of Puglia provide opportunities for mindfulness and relaxation. Unplug, relax, and take in the beauty of nature all around you.

- Engage in age-old wellness techniques like yoga, which are increasingly available in many cities and resorts. These methods offer a holistic view of wellbeing.

- Wellness retreats and spa resorts in Puglia include procedures, therapies, and exercises intended to revive and repair.

Keeping Healthy While Travelling

- Puglia's warm temperature necessitates maintaining adequate hydration. Keep a reusable water bottle with you and sip frequently, especially when you're outside.

- The sun in Puglia can be harsh. To protect oneself from UV rays, put on sunscreen, a hat, and sturdy clothing.

- Olive oil from Puglia is well known for its therapeutic properties. Enjoy its distinctive flavour by incorporating it into your dishes.

- Pay attention to seasonal health issues and allergies. If you have any particular sensitivity, speak with your healthcare practitioner.

- Get enough rest and sleep to maintain a healthy immune system and enough energy for exploration.

- Keep a list of all the hospitals, clinics, and pharmacies in your area for quick access.

Puglia is the perfect location for a wellness-focused vacation due to its all-natural beauty, wholesome cuisine, and chances for leisure and activity. You may maximise your travels while taking care of your health in this alluring area by adopting a balanced lifestyle and being ready for any health-related demands.

Currency and Finances

For a seamless and stress-free trip, navigating the financial landscape while travelling is crucial. Understanding the local currency, managing your money, and using financial services are essential for having a good trip in Puglia, as they are in any location.

The Euro (€) is the country's official currency, which includes Puglia. To prevent confusion during transactions, it's essential to become familiar with the denominations of Euro coins and notes as well as their appearance.

The following coins are available in 1 Euro: 1 cent, 2 cents, 5 cents, 10 cents, 20 cents, and 50 cents.

Euro bills come in the following denominations: 5, 10, 20, 50, 100, 200, and 500 euros.

Payment Options

Cash

Puglia accepts a lot of cash. It is preferable to keep small bills on hand for daily costs and larger bills on hand for larger purchases.

Cards, including credit and debit

In restaurants, hotels, shops, and other larger venues, credit and debit cards are routinely accepted. The most widely used credit card kinds are Visa and MasterCard, followed by American Express and Diners Club, both of which may have less widespread acceptance.

Automated Teller Machines (ATMs)

These machines are extensively dispersed throughout cities and towns. They provide a practical way for you to use your debit or credit card to get cash in the local currency.

Exchange and Conversion of Currencies

Exchange Bureaus

While there are choices for converting foreign currency to euros in major cities like Bari and Lecce, currency exchange offices are less popular in smaller towns.

Banks

Banks can help with currency exchange, however they frequently charge more than exchange bureaus do. They might, however, offer additional dependability and security.

Budgeting and Financial Management

Plan Ahead

Prior to your vacation, calculate your daily costs and make a budget. Include the cost of your lodging, meals, transportation, admissions, and any planned activities.

Regional Food

Local markets and restaurants in Puglia offer delectable meals at reasonable prices. To save money and taste real flavours, embrace regional food.

Tipping

In Puglia, tipping is encouraged but not required. The bill might already include a service fee. If not, a little gratuity is a nice way to show your appreciation.

Unreported Fees

Some banks and credit card issuers may charge foreign transaction fees when using credit cards outside of the country. Before your vacation, inquire about these fees with your bank.

Emergency Funds

Keep a little local money on hand in case of unforeseen circumstances where cards might not be accepted.

Apps

Install currency conversion apps on your phone to get real-time exchange rates and assist you in making wise financial decisions.

Financial Services

In Puglia, banks normally have morning hours from Monday through Friday (often 8:30 AM to 1:30 PM), and some also have restricted hours on Saturdays.

ATMs are the easiest way to withdraw money. To ensure secure transactions, utilise ATMs connected to recognised banks.

To avoid paying Dynamic Currency Conversion (DCC) costs, make sure you choose the local currency option while using ATMs.

The financial system and currency of Puglia guarantee that visitors have a variety of options for handling their money. You may concentrate on enjoying your tour through this interesting region while maintaining control over your funds by being aware of local payment options, setting sensible spending limits, and comprehending currency conversion.

Time

In Puglia, time moves at a pace that perfectly complements the region's serene surroundings, fascinating past, and lively culture. Immersing oneself in the culture requires that you comprehend the local understanding of time, which includes time zones, business hours, and the practise of savouring each minute.

Central European Time (CET), which is observed in Puglia, runs from UTC+1 during normal time to UTC+2 during daylight saving time. To properly schedule your activities, meetings, and travel plans, you must be informed of the local time zone.

Hours of Operation

In Puglia, working hours frequently reflect the relaxed and easygoing way of life in the region. The general breakdown of business hours is as follows:

- Smaller towns frequently have stores that close for a siesta for a few hours in the afternoon (typically from 1:00 to 4:00 PM), then reopen until 8:00 PM, but larger cities may have more regular hours.

- In Puglia, lunch is a big meal that is normally served from 12:30 PM to 3 PM. Around 8:00 PM, dinner service begins, and it may go late into the night.

- In the off-season, cultural institutions like museums and historical sites frequently close on Mondays and may operate with fewer hours. Extended hours could be provided in the summer.

- Banks typically are open from Monday through Friday from 8:30 am to 1:30 pm in the morning. On Saturdays, some people might provide fewer services.

- Post offices normally operate during bank hours, with Saturday services being somewhat constrained.

Knowing the time zones help to ensure that your journey to Puglia is rich and memorable.

Internet Connection

Staying connected is crucial for communication, navigation, and sharing your experiences in Puglia with the rest of the globe in the current age of travel. A dependable internet connection improves your journey by helping you plan your itinerary and identify the best nearby restaurants. Here is an overview of Puglia's internet connectivity.

SIM Cards and Mobile Data

Consider getting a local SIM card from a company like TIM, Vodafone, or Wind once you are in Puglia.

By doing this, you can access data and have a local phone number without paying exorbitant international roaming fees.

SIM cards can be purchased at carrier outlets, convenience stores, and airports. Before purchasing an international SIM card, make sure your phone is unlocked.

Various data packages are available from mobile carriers to meet a range of demands, from short-term traveller plans to longer-term choices. Find a plan that meets your data needs by doing some research.

Wi-Fi

The majority of Puglian hotels, resorts, and guesthouses provide free Wi-Fi to visitors. When you check in, ask your hotel provider about the Wi-Fi password and availability.

Customers can use free Wi-Fi in a large number of bars, cafes, and restaurants. Wi-Fi access codes are frequently supplied upon request or displayed conspicuously.

Free public Wi-Fi may be available in some public areas, including parks, plazas, and libraries. Keep an eye out for indications suggesting the presence of such services.

Major towns may provide tourist information centres with free Wi-Fi for guests. While getting online, it's a good idea to swing by for maps and neighbourhood information.

Useful Advice for Efficient Internet Access

While remote rural places may have poor network access, urban areas often have high network coverage. Consequently, schedule your interactions and communications.

Utilise your phone's built-in data consumption tracking tools or download third-party apps to keep an eye on your data usage and prevent going over your plan's data allotment.

Download Puglia offline maps using apps like Google Maps before going anywhere. Because of this, you can navigate even when you aren't online.

Use VoIP and messaging apps to make free or inexpensive calls and have video chats via Wi-Fi. Examples of VoIP apps are WhatsApp, Skype, and Zoom.

To make sure you stay connected all day, keep your devices fully charged and carry a portable charger.

To keep your data secure when utilising public Wi-Fi networks, think about using a virtual private network (VPN).

Cultural Protocols and Etiquette

For an authentic and respectful trip, it is essential to comprehend and abide by Puglian cultural customs. Accepting cultural norms enhances your experience and creates lasting bonds as you tour the area's quaint towns, mingle with the populace, and participate in its customs.

Greetings and Interactions

Pugliese and other Italians cherish friendliness and warmth in their dealings. As you enter stores, cafes, and other facilities, smile and say "buongiorno" (good morning) or "buonasera" (good evening) to the people.

Secondly, Italians are renowned for their adoring actions, such as kisses on the cheek. It's preferable to wait for the other person to start these motions, though. Keep to the proper personal space until you become accustomed to the customs.

Also note that the use of hand gestures is essential to communication in Italian. Even though some gestures may look familiar, you should refrain from imitating them unless you are certain of their intent.

Respectful Attire and Appearance.

Even on informal outings, Pugliese people frequently dress nicely. Whether you're visiting historical landmarks or enjoying a meal at a neighbourhood trattoria, dress neatly and cleanly for the occasion.

As a sign of respect, keep your shoulders and knees covered when entering churches or other religious buildings. For these situations, a shawl or scarf can be a useful addition.

Dining Etiquette

In Puglia, lunch is a filling meal that is frequently had between 12:30 PM and 3:00 PM. Dinner is served later, typically at or after 8:00 PM.

Pugliese people eat slowly, enjoying each dish, and conversing with one another. Accept this leisurely way of dining.

It is usual to hold off on starting to dine until the host sets the table or makes a toast. Additionally, avoid resting your elbows on the table and keep your hands visible.

Accept Puglia's gastronomic offers when dining out. Asking for recommendations from locals and trying regional specialties are both quite acceptable.

Sites and Traditions of Culture

Speak quietly and follow any clothing standards when entering churches or other places of worship. In these areas, avoid utilising flash photography.

The municipalities of Puglia frequently have their own distinctive traditions and customs. Pay attention to and adhere to regional customs, particularly at festivals and celebrations.

Gifts and Gratuities

It's nice to bring a small present, such as a bottle of local wine, cookies, or flowers, if you've been asked to go to someone's home.

Even though there may be a service charge on the bill, giving a small tip is always appreciated. It's customary to round up the cost or add an extra 5% to 10%.

Knowing Siesta

Similar to other regions of Italy, Puglia observes "siesta," a midday break during which stores, eateries, and other enterprises may close for a while. This is the ideal time to relax, have a leisurely supper, or visit indoor attractions.

The cultural environment of Puglia is a synthesis of customs, influences, and histories. Accept this diversity with an open mind and a desire to discover other cultures' traditions and viewpoints.

You'll develop closer ties, promote respect for one another, and make priceless memories by immersing yourself in Puglia's cultural customs and traditions. Keep in mind that genuine curiosity, friendliness, and an openness to change can go a long way towards making your trip to Puglia both enriching and unforgettable.

CONCLUSION

We hope you enjoy your journey through the enthralling landscapes, rich history, vibrant culture, and welcoming people of this alluring region. With its sandy coastline, quaint towns, and mouthwatering cuisine, Puglia will weave itself into your heart and leave you with memories that you will cherish long after you have left.

Puglia invites you to slow down, appreciate each moment, and genuinely connect with the region's soul by adopting a different rhythm for time. Every turn exposes a tale waiting to be found, from the azure Adriatic waters to the sun-drenched olive fields.

Puglia's distinctive identity is woven together from the region's exquisite architecture, the perfume of freshly made bread, and the laughter shared over a leisurely lunch.

It doesn't matter if you're wandering the white-washed alleyways of Ostuni, admiring the historic trulli in Alberobello, or simply enjoying the breathtaking cliffside views in Polignano a Mare, your trip to Puglia will be one of cultural enrichment and genuine connections.

The heart of this region lies in the unexpected moments, the laughter shared with locals, the warmth of a welcoming smile, and the breath-taking vistas. Let your memories of Puglia serve as a constant reminder that travelling isn't just about seeing new locations, it's also about the relationships you create, the tales you gather, and the internal changes you experience.

May your heart be overflowing with thankfulness as you say goodbye to Puglia for the experiences you've had, the connections you've made, and the beauty that has touched your spirit. You will always have a special place in your heart for Puglia, and we can't wait to greet you once more when you decide to come back.

Until then, may your journey be chock-full of excitement, joy, and the spirit of exploration.

Buon viaggio!!

Evelyn Blair.

Ps: If you love this book and you're also looking to visit Amsterdam, Netherlands, you can also get the book "Amsterdam Travel Guide 2023" by Evelyn Blair here
If you're looking to visit Denver as well, you can get the book "Denver Travel Guide 2023" by Evelyn Blair here

Made in United States
Orlando, FL
07 September 2023

36789120R00117